30 - 77

The Limits
of
Nuclear War

*THINKING ABOUT
THE DO-ABLE
AND THE UN-DO-ABLE*

by Paul Ramsey

Published by
The Council on Religion and International Affairs

Copyright 1963 by
THE COUNCIL ON RELIGION AND INTERNATIONAL AFFAIRS
170 East 64th Street, New York, N. Y. 10021
Third Printing 1970

All rights reserved
Printed in the United States of America
Library of Congress No. 63-17701

FOREWORD

Some of the most crucial political and moral questions of our time flow directly from the development of modern weapons of mass destruction. The questions are urgent, they are hard, they are complex — and they remain largely unanswered. In recent years the Council on Religion and International Affairs has devoted a major part of its program of seminars, consultations and publications to exactly these questions. The purpose of the Council has been to sharpen, to clarify and, possibly, to propose answers for responsible consideration.

One of the persons who has contributed most generously to this effort is Paul Ramsey. He has addressed himself with energy and intellectual rigor to the ethical problems created by modern weapons. With this essay, "The Limits of Nuclear War," he goes a significant step beyond his *War and the Christian Conscience* in the analysis of the moral issues involved in nuclear deterrence.

Dr. Ramsey is Harrington Spear Paine Professor of Christian Ethics at Princeton University. He is the author of *War and the Christian Conscience,* written under the auspices of the Lilly Endowment Research Program in Christianity and Politics, and more recently, *The Just War: Force and Political Responsibility.*

JAMES FINN
Director of Publications

The Council on Religion
and International Affairs

3

CONTENTS

The Context of the Problem

The writing of this paper was begun in the context of a deeply distressing event. For seventeen years of the nuclear age no leader of the Western world indicated any doubt that military policy should be based on President Truman's judgment that an entire city is a legitimate military target. The "massive" deterrence of the Dulles era, when the United States still had a monopoly of atomic weapons, has now been supplanted by "balanced" deterrence from hopefully invulnerable bases. Arms control and measures to lessen the danger of surprise attack and of accidental war have been proposed, and conventional and "unconventional" military capabilities have been strengthened. But during these years there appeared to be no crack in the official acceptance of cities as targets for total destruction.

Then in June, 1962, Secretary of Defense Robert McNamara delivered the commencement address of the University of Michigan. In this speech, which had the approval of President Kennedy, he said: "The United States has come to the conclusion that, to the extent feasible, basic military strategy in a possible nuclear war should be approached in much the same way that more conventional military operations have been regarded in the past. That is to say, principal military objectives, in the event of a nuclear war stemming from an attack on the Alliance, should be the destruction of the enemy's forces, not of his civilian population."

Instead of a chorus of "Amens!" from the millions of decent citizens of this country, Christian and non-Christian, hardly a single voice was raised to say, "*That* is certainly the upper limit of what we ever want done in our behalf, if for no other reason than that it is clearly the upper limit of what can ever be done in defense of anything." Hardly a "civilized" person was reminded by the Secretary's words that the proscription of direct attack upon a whole society is the oldest and most well-established rule of civilized warfare. Hardly a Christian was reminded by the Secretary's words to seek from his own traditional teachings practical wisdom for the direction of public affairs. Hardly any of the leaders of religious and public opinion stepped forward to support the most significant change (or suggestion of change) in military policy in nearly two decades of the nuclear age.

Instead, the opinions expressed were stereotyped and evidenced as much inertia as can exist in the vast and sprawling defense establishment which McNamara is struggling to subdue and direct. Perhaps resistance to McNamara's proposal was to be expected from our allies.[1] When we think of the magnitude and complexities of our interlocking systems of defense, "doctrine" is almost bound to lag behind realities. It is not surprising, therefore, that C. L. Sulzberger reported from London that this novel "nuclear defense theory, based on counterforce rather than countercity strategy . . . produced confused reactions in Europe," or that he concluded two weeks after the policy was announced: "It is now dead."[2] Yet it is surprising, and most distressing that individual leaders of opinion manifest not much greater freedom to explore "new" doctrine.

Instead of support for this or any other effort to limit the nuclear holocaust for which the two great powers now stand ready, one heard only sterile protests that our leaders were again trying to make us grow "accustomed" to the idea of fighting a nuclear war. Instead of applauding the announcement as a policy of definitely *limited* feasibility, the public widely regarded it as simply one more assertion of the limited *feasibility* of nuclear war. Even the *Christian Century* damned with faint praise — because the editors apparently know in advance that any thoughtful effort to un-target the cities is bound to prove impossible. It will show "the essentially unmanageable nature of these weapons," and direct us again with single-minded attention to "the importance of preventing any war from starting."

"So vast is the destructive capacity of nuclear weapons that their effects could not be confined to military objects," said the *Century*, sweeping aside any distinction between effects that cannot be confined and deliberately enlarging those effects by targeting on cities. "Would the United States," it asked rhetorically, "be prepared to remove military installations from the vicinity of its great cities, where some of them are now located?" — as if war plans must now and for the future be ruled by the stupidity of Congressmen who secure the location of missile bases in their districts near large centers of population where there is an unemployment problem; and as if the fact that Tucson, Arizona and Plattsburg, New York and Omaha, Nebraska and Colorado Springs,

---

[1]*The New York Times* reported (August 9, 1962) that Franz Josef Strauss, West German Defense Minister, "'is giving up hard' on a strategy based largely on nuclear weapons." Herr Strauss apparently believes not so much in a credible fight-the-war policy as in deterrence that "begins at the battle line" with tactical nuclear weapons and goes to the grave line, by means of massive nuclear weapons targeted mainly on cities.

[2]*The New York Times*, July 9, 1962.

8

Colorado are now legitimate military targets means that this must necessarily remain the shape of modern war. "In making his proposal Mr. McNamara has rendered a service," the *Century* concluded, "but probably not the one he intended to render. What he has really done — or so we hope — is to strengthen the argument of the Committee for a Sane Nuclear Policy that the only safe way to manage nuclear weapons is to abolish them as one step in a plan of complete disarmament."[3]

The Alternatives of Policy

So far public opinion in this country seems to ignore the difference between 25,000,000 dead as the probable result of all-out counterforce warfare and 215,000,000 dead as a result of all-out countercity warfare between the great powers.[4] We seem to turn away from any effort to make counterforce nuclear war, if it comes, fall far, far short of all-out. So, in addition, do we gloss over the qualitative moral distinction between tragically killing or sacrificing human beings as an indirect result of knocking out military targets (counterforce warfare) and the murderous policy of deliberately killing them in totally devastating countercity warfare. The only ground for hope is that our leaders who must make the decisions will not be so irresponsible. Richard Fryklund reports, at least, that the shift to counterforces strategy has been in the making for the duration of this administration, and he always writes of the decision in the past tense.[5]

Still, this is a decision that will have to be not only our actual policy but our *declared* policy. More than once it will have to be declared, and massive manifold actions will have to be taken in accord with it, if there is again to be a well-understood boundary and a mutually accepted limit in the conduct of war. This will require the support of an informed and morally sensitive people. When one asks why the just conduct of war is the last thing people want to talk about or to believe possible, or why they do not demand that governments make only limited nuclear war possible (if there is to be nuclear war) or limited war (if there is to be war at all), the answers are hard to give except in terms of a breakdown of the tradition of civilized politics that is without parallel.

Yet these distinctions among possible strategies have long been made by weapons analysts. Glenn H. Snyder, for example, discusses at

---

[3]Editorial, July 4, 1962.
[4]C. L. Sulzberger's report, *op. cit.*, of the estimates on which McNamara's policy shift was based. These, of course, are very uncertain figures.
[5]*100 Million Lives: Maximum Survival in a Nuclear Age,* New York: The Macmillan Co., 1962. The Pentagon studies and debates go back to early 1960.

some length the choice between "all-out counter*city* retaliation" and "all-out counter*force* retaliation," and also between "*limited* counter*city* retaliation as a bargaining tactic" and "*limited* counter*force* retaliation."[6] And Herman Kahn's latest book spells out in some detail the difference that exists and *can* be drawn between "Counterforce plus Countervalue," "Straight Counterforce," "Counterforce and Bonus," and "Counterforce plus Avoidance" in the choice of strategies.[7] Moreover, two other such books have recently appeared: one analyzes "limited strategic warfare";[8] the other, based in part on interviews with highly-placed Pentagon officials, offers a reporter's analysis of a "No City" strategy (Kahn's "Straight Counterforce" or "Counterforce plus Avoidance") in contrast to "Pure City," "Cities Plus" or "Devastation" war-plans.[9]

Thus, there stands on one side Countervalue warfare; Pure City, Cities Plus and Devastation war; controlled or unlimited Countercity retaliation; Counterforce plus Countervalue or Counterforce and Bonus; and limited strategic city reprisal. These all aim at civilians, except for the sort of "countervalue" warfare which proposes to allow time for cities to be evacuated. On the other side stands Counterforce warfare; No City war; controlled or unlimited Counterforce retaliation; Straight Counterforce or Counterforce plus Avoidance. Only Counterforce plus Avoidance may be called a just way to conduct war, since traditional and acceptable moral teachings concerning legitimate military targets require the avoidance of civilian damage as much as possible even while accepting this as in some measure an unavoidable indirect effect.

This paper defends the thesis that counterforce nuclear war is the upper limit of rational, politically purposive military action. Two ways are commonly taken to avoid this conclusion, and another uncommonly. Those who magnify the difficulty and undesirability of adopting a policy of making just war possible usually do so because:

(1) they believe that general disarmament is about to be accomplished and therefore no plans should be made for the use of any weapons, nuclear or other; or else because

(2) they believe that balanced deterrence can be stabilized and kept perfect enough to insure that nuclear weapons will never be used except in their non-use for deterrence.

---

[6]*Deterrence and Defense*, Princeton, N. J.: Princeton University Press, 1961, pp. 68-79.

[7]*Thinking about the Unthinkable*, New York: Horizon Press, 1962, pp. 65-68.

[8]Klaus Knorr and Thornton Read, eds., *Limited Strategic War*, New York: Praeger, 1962. In this volume, this concept includes both limited strategic city reprisal and limited strategic attacks on forces.

[9]Richard Fryklund: *100 Million Lives: Maximum Survival in a Nuclear War.* New York: The Macmillan Co., 1962.

In these two schools, extremes meet. They are brothers under the skin who believe so strongly in peace by disarmament (whether unilaterally or by treaty or by technical contrivance by which the weapons will neutralize themselves) that as a consequence they see no need for thinking about the upper limit of sanity in the actual use of nuclear weapons. The conclusion that "Pure City" is the only way in which nuclear war can ever be fought, or the judgment that "Pure City" is the aim the weapons *should* have, is thus "the favorite [strategy] of influential civilians whose eyes are actually on disarmament rather than defense,"[10] or who, at least, find it impossible to be active on two political fronts at once. And not only civilians.[11] Even Prussians are pacifists of this new breed. So Franz Josef Strauss, West German Defense Minister, explained why he did not want even to *discuss* plans that actually exist for controlled fighting in Europe by saying that the inevitable outcome would be that "the credibility of the deterrent is weakened. . . . And if we do not have a deterrent that is credible, the only alternative is war as an element of policy."[12]

Therefore, no steps *should* be taken to plan to fight war justly against forces if you believe that peace by deliberate disarmament can soon be achieved; and no such steps *need* be taken if you believe that weapons technology can keep the nations permanently disarmed and no future rational decision-maker need ever decide to fire these weapons. Most, if not quite all, of the arguments against counterforces warfare (its instability, for example) have absolute peace as their premise; and the latter is, one way or another, believed to be a genuine, and the sole, option today.[13] There is an inner logical connection between indigenous American pacifism and the Strategic Air Command with its motto, "Peace is our profession." "Pacifistic deterrence" has been our policy, our hope and our faith. Only if fighting a possible war is understood to be a governing purpose of a military establishment will inherent limits in the design of war seem choiceworthy. It is always easier to plan murder and mutual suicide, and somehow despairingly more pleasant too, than to plan for defense and the survival of the nation.

---

[10]Fryklund, *op. cit.*, p. 42.

[11]Cf. General Pierre Gallois: *The Balance of Terror: Strategy for the Nuclear Age.* Boston, Mass.: Houghton Mifflin Co., 1961.

[12]*The New York Times,* March 1, 1962.

[13]For this argument in expanded form, see my "Dream and Reality in Deterrence and Defense," *Christianity and Crisis,* vol. xxi, no. 22 (Dec. 25, 1961), pp. 228-232; "U.S. Military Policy and 'Shelter Morality,'" *worldview,* vol. 5, no. 1 (Jan., 1962), pp. 6-9; "Correspondence," *worldview,* vol. 5, no. 3 (March, 1962), pp. 6-9; "Turn Toward Just War," *worldview,* vol. 5, nos. 7-8 (July-August, 1962), pp. 8-13; and *War and the Christian Conscience,* Durham, N. C.: Duke University Press, 1961.

There is no way to avoid thinking about militarily feasible and politically purposive warfare. Against the first of these positions, it must be said that nuclear weapons and armaments in general are unlikely to be scrapped soon, if ever. Against the second, it must be said that "balanced" deterrence and invulnerable weapons-systems do not preclude the need to think about believable fight-the-war plans. Instead, the opposite is the result. The more the great powers think they have achieved for the moment a nearly automatic neutralization of nuclear weapons, from bases it will take years to find a way of attacking, the more the world is prepared for local war, for conventional and unconventional war. The more, too, will it seem possible to make a controlled use of tactical nuclears, and after that to expand the war to controlled attacks upon an enemy's strategic forces and then to engage with him in a cold-blooded exchange of a few cities.

The third, and more uncommon way, of going around or beyond counterforces warfare is to envision a slow-lobbing intercity exchange as, under some circumstances, the decision of statesmanship. It is this proposal of "limited attacks on cities," or "controlled countervalue" war or "Counterforce plus Bonus civilian damage," which should be examined in depth. In doing so, I shall regard the limited exchange of cities as a lower limit of Pure City or of unlimited Countervalue war, and not as simply a variant or upper limit of controlled (or even all-out) Counterforces warfare. Those analysts who fail to note here an essential distinction have failed to observe the point at which, in making a courageous effort to "think about the unthinkable," they themselves began to think about the un-do-able.

Herman Kahn's latest book, *Thinking about the Unthinkable*, bears in its title reference to the contribution for which we are all indebted to him and to other weapons analysts. Some actions and events have been termed "unthinkable" because they are unpleasant to consider, or because they disturb our customary ways of thinking, or because we are weak in our determination to overcome the problem and submit it to the most rigorous rational analysis. Other proposed actions, however, are "unthinkable" in the far different and deeper sense that they are morally or politically "un-do-able." Properly to think about the unthinkable requires that we be open to the possibility that such effort will lead beyond the mere delineation of many possibilities for choice and action, which are distinguishable only extrinsically and in terms of consequences. That man is not quite resolute in thinking about the unthinkable who does not know that he may one day think something that is, in and of itself, un-do-able. He has not much confidence in his own powers of rational analysis who does not know that he can perfectly well think the "unthinkable" which will remain unthinkable in the sense that it is, for human agency, un-do-able.

A first illustration of this is to be found in what analysts say about policies based on the "rationality of irrationality." There is a point where a fundamental irrationality of at least some of these policies becomes evident in the fact that, we are told, one must irrevocably "commit" himself to doing them. That is to say, there are some actions that cannot be *done* at the time they are to occur. For them to occur, human agency and rationality must be placed in suspense at the time of occurrence. One must get himself bound by some artistic contrivance, or, better still, by acting as if he were a force of nature, before the event happens or before the (wrongly termed) "action" is to take place. "Committal strategies" cannot, in the extreme instances, be located in the ethical and political sphere. Instead, ethics and politics are abolished by the adoption of such strategies, for the simple reason that they put human agency out of commission. They are designed to do precisely this.

In this day when action and the principles of right action have been so far reduced to techniques, Aristotle's distinction between "making" and "doing" reasserts itself at the heart of any consideration of "committal strategies." "Making," he said, always has "something beyond itself" as an objective, whether this be a poem, a physical artifact, a weapons system or a social system. In contrast, in ethics and politics, "the very well-doing is in itself an End."[14] Right and wrong doing are to be found in the nature of moral and political agency itself, and not first of all in any of its external results. Of course, from any "well-doing" a lot of "making" results. Even so these are not the same.

The fundamental questions of ethics and politics have to do with "the very well-doing" that in and of itself is an end and norm of action. This question is simply avoided by schemes that plainly annul human agency at the place and time of an event's occurrence. Extreme "committal strategies" cannot be the result of an exercise of practical reason which Aristotle rightly called "doing." As un-do-able actions, they can only be contrived by "Art," an exercise of practical reason properly called "making"; or, we might say today, as a consequence of social "engineering." Today, those who manage to think the un-do-able actionable, accomplish this in large measure by virtue of what Jacques Maritain calls a "merely artistic view of politics" and of military conduct.

I once improved on Herman Kahn's use of the game of "Chicken!" as an analogy to the game of deterrence. The driver who wants to make *certain* he will win this game (to "deter" the other driver and force him to pull over before their vehicles collide) can do so by being the *first*

---

[14]*Nichomachean Ethics,* 1140b.

to strap his steering wheel and communicate to his opponent that he has done so and now *cannot* pull over even if he wanted to do so.[15] This is how one must contrive to do the un-do-able. He must effectively rule out human choice and agency at the time a totally irrational action is to be produced. He must get himself totally committed, and he is not totally committed if any "doing" remains to be done. Neither at the time of deterrence *nor before* has he made a human *political* decision, or chosen means apt to political ends if used, or put forth a political deed. *Before,* he did an *artistic* thing, beautiful to behold, whose whole meaning was to rule out choice and to make the exercise of political wisdom impossible at that later moment. This is the only way to think, and to think how to do, the un-do-able.

Now I find Kahn saying this same thing more clearly than in his earlier book, in which he stated that "Doomsday" deterrence machines would be unchoiceworthy (un-do-able) even if they might work. Or, rather, I find him stepping back and forth across the line between the unthinkable that has not yet clearly been thought and the unthinkable that, the more you think about it *with political judgment,* is inherently un-do-able. Out of his own writings our present point can best be made, namely, that this line exists between right and wrong political choice, and it is not one to be discovered merely by calculating numbers killed or saved or by engineering the values marched by in various scenarios. It is, rather, in the mind and judgment of the observer stimulated by "War and Peace Games" to think about "doing" and what is worthy to be done, as a just man would make the choice and perform the deed. Scenarios and "War and Peace Games" are altogether to be praised for what they can do to enlarge our knowledge of actual and exceedingly complex cases moving, as they must, through time. They stimulate the imagination, and if in no other way the opposing "team" insures that no fact or riposte or consequence is neglected.[16] This has always been the service of actual or hypothetical "cases" in moral and political

---

[15]In John C. Bennett, ed.: *Nuclear Weapons and the Conflict of Conscience.* New York: Chas. Scribner's Sons, 1962, p. 166.

[16]Litigation in our law courts and our "adversary" procedure are also ways of re-enacting the case and making sure that all the relevant facts will be found and brought to bear upon the decision. Here, however, members of the jury, deciding as to the facts of the case, also bring their sense of justice and injustice to bear on it; and rules of law, in which they are instructed by the judge, are not only positive laws "making" right but also depositories of collective judgment as to the justice or injustice of similar cases, and judge-made law provides a growing edge of decision-making in which the justice or injustice of a specific aggregation of personal and impersonal facts is determined. It is one thing to mount procedures apt in determining facts and for thinking the unthinkable action one is enabled and almost forced by these procedures to think through concretely. It is another thing to judge that the unthinkable is criminal. War and Peace Games-men should remember this.

reasoning: they require and enable informed concrete decision to be made. But, in an earlier age, this exercise was for the purpose of illuminating and stimulating *judgment* concerning what is to be done or not done, and not only to enable a man to think something about some "unthinkable" situation that might possibly face him in the future. Since Herman Kahn has probably run through more scenarios than anyone else, and since he is also a moral man concerned with the conduct of politics and war, it is helpful to observe him making judgments concerning the to-be-done and the not-to-be-done.

Before examining his position, I will insert here the opinion that the morality of war, and distinctions between just and unjust, rational and irrational, human and inhuman conduct, would be clearer in Kahn's writings if these distinctions were not trammelled from the beginning, and turned into seemingly *technical* judgments only, by the conviction he shares with most modern men that since war as such is immoral, no *moral* judgments can be made concerning the way it is conducted. In short, if there is no distinction to be made between killing and murder in the calculated (*vs.* wanton) acts of war between nations, then only technical questions remain to be solved. For example, the *numbers* the computers tell us will be dead will be the only basis for choice between, say, counterforces warfare and limited strategic city exchanges for bargaining purposes.

"Rationality of irrationality" policies cannot be said to be useless in politics. It was certainly true that, in the case of many delegates to the U.N., "the apprehensions created by Mr. Khrushchev's boorish actions in the General Assembly outweighed their dislike of such behavior," and that these delegates became "more disposed to go along with Soviet demands."[17] Nevertheless, *extreme* "rationality of irrationality" policies obviously become irrational again. For a nation to go to *total* committal policies is obviously to step over the line into action by contrivance, despite the fact that the action is politically un-do-able. Total committal to irrational action turns diplomacy or statesmanship itself into a Doomsday machine whose parts are erstwhile people.

This, it seems to me, Kahn now says more clearly. He spells out more fully what it would take to deter irrational action by irrational action. One must say convincingly, "One of us has to be reasonable and it is not going to be me, so it has to be you."[18] "One of us has to be responsible and it isn't going to be me, so it has to be you."[19] Now, how can this be done effectively, and effectively communicated? The enemy

[17]Thomas J. Hamilton in *The New York Times,* Oct. 30, 1960.
[18]Kahn, *op. cit.,* p. 78.
[19]*Ibid.,* p. 130.

has to be convinced you are "stark, staring mad"[20] or

totally reckless, oblivious to the danger, out of control. These objectives can probably be met best by getting into the car drunk, wearing very dark glasses, and conspicuously throwing the steering wheel out of the window as soon as the car has gotten up speed.[21]

The side using this tactic tries to act like an unreasoning force of nature or, at least, a rigid human being. It tries to point out, implicitly or explicitly, that, "One does not argue with a hurricane, one seeks shelter in a cellar or suffers the consequence. Why then do you argue with me?" This tactic is particularly effective upon bystanders.[22]

Yet Kahn knows that this cannot be *done*, certainly not by a free society or by a government responsive to the will and responsible for the weal of a free society. He writes that

thermonuclear threats . . . must look and be both prudent and rational. We cannot go around threatening to blow up a major portion of the world, or attempt to get our way by looking insane and dauntless. These strategies might be available to a totalitarian nation. They are not available to us, a democratic nation in a democratic alliance. Strategies overly dependent on resolve, on committing first, on extreme use of the rationality of irrationality, are not likely to succeed if attempted by the West.[23]

And immediately after one of Kahn's most extreme statements of how "best" to play this game of deterrence by total committal, he writes:

If we must play the game, we should play it soberly, with clear vision, and in full control of both our capabilities and our emotions, even if doing this results in serious competitive disadvantages. We must do this in order to have both the appearance and reality of responsible leadership.[24]

In both the foregoing passages, Kahn plainly calls for never *being* or *appearing* to be totally committed to action that is so irrational it can never be politically done by free and present decision. Certainly, the upper limit of the politically do-able would be to appear to have strapped the wheel or thrown it away, but not actually to do so. Given the *deterrent* value of "this *appearance* of irrationally inexorable commitment," one would want to provide for the possibility of revoking the apparently irrevocable, since "if deterrence fails . . . it would then be

[20] *Ibid.*, p. 79.
[21] *Ibid.*, p. 45. Also see p. 188. "The youthful degenerates' game would be a better analogy if it were played with two cars at an unknown distance apart, travelling towards each other at an unknown speed, and on roads with a fork or two so that one is not even certain that he is on the same road as his opponent" (*ibid.*, p. 187).
[22] *Ibid.*, p. 179.
[23] *Ibid.*, p. 124.
[24] *Ibid.*, pp. 188-9.

irrational to carry through the commitment."[25] There may even be "some advantage in not using too extreme a 'rationality of irrationality' strategy," because, if you neither are nor seem to be totally committed, the enemy may actually do only what *he* can do purposefully, then and there at the time of action.[26]

Still there are passages in his recent book in which Kahn seems to hold open for adoption strategies which he himself has plainly stated ought never to be chosen, and which, his own analysis makes clear, *cannot* be "done" except by "making" ourselves do them (if that is to be called "doing"). He writes, for example, "*It can make sense* to commit oneself irrevocably to do something in a particular eventuality, and at the same time it may not make sense to carry out the commitment if the eventuality occurs."[27] Yet far more frequently, as I have shown, Kahn says *this cannot make sense*. Certainly not the actuality of it, and likely not the appearance either. This is not surprising, for we should have known all along that rational purposive action cannot contradict itself, or ever be "made" to do so. "Making" cannot take the place of "doing," nor contrivance replace responsible decision in the moment of action, nor can Art supplant Politics, if men remain men.

War as a Test of Wills

Policies of extreme committal to irrational behavior are only one illustration of where one is driven when war is regarded as primarily or exclusively a trial of wills or a test of resolve. There is no end here, no limits. Limited strategic war involving controlled city exchanges or limited countercity retaliation *as a bargaining tactic* offer another illustration of war in which the sides aim to "prevail" by demonstrating resolution. This, too, is "unthinkable" in the sense that the more you think about it the more it will seem manifestly "un-do-able." But first, a word should be said about war as a trial of wills in contrast to war as a trial of strength.

In war as a trial of wills, what one side does is determined primarily by its calculation of what the other side expects of it, or what is required for its resolution to be broken. Analysts in our day have developed an entire science of purely voluntaristic games of strategy simply by abstracting the encounter of the wills and minds of the

---

[25]*Ibid.*, p. 68.
[26]*Ibid.*, p. 69.
[27]*Ibid.*, p. 45 (italics mine).

combatants (always a significant aspect of military engagements) from other factors. Put aside for purposes of analysis are considerations of war as a resort to a controlled collision of bodily forces, war as a trial of physical strength, or war as the challenge and response of national entities each with concrete policies to be defended or effected. Where will and resolve are at issue, the question is not what would I do if I were the enemy seeking to enforce some definite national policy by possible resort to arms. The question is rather: What would I do if I were he, wondering what he should do if he were wondering what I would do if I were he . . .? In the determination of radically voluntaristic policy, the focal point is each side's expectation of what the other expects it to expect to be expected to do. Such is the result of our present-day attempt thoroughly to "spiritualize" the conduct of war. Such is the result of trying to elevate war from being a trial of strength directed toward some controlling objective, and of transmuting it into a test of resolve which has no other purpose than to prove who wins in a battle of wills. There is no limit or end to this. One is guided only by "what he expects the other to do, knowing that the other is similarly guided, so that each is aware that each must try to guess what the second guesses the first will guess the second to guess and so on, in the familiar spiral of reciprocal expectations."[28]

Much of the language of the foregoing paragraph presupposes that a nation's strategy is framed as a *response*, though an empty response that takes shape only, or mainly, in terms of what it expects another (so far) empty expectation to expect of it. You have the same conflict of wills, each empty and formless until it is filled by the other, if it is supposed that one is on the "offensive," trying to "bargain" with the other, to break his resolution, or to deter him from further action. Thus, the determination of strategy takes place almost wholly within a meeting of the wills and resolves of the combatants, in the sense that what each must be willing to do in order to "win" is determined by what the other is willing to do. This goes on to mutual destruction, or until one gives up and turns away, or until the strange notion comes to the mind of one or both of them that warfare has no limit or purpose unless it is predominantly a trial of strength.

American voluntarism was the source of this nation's confidence in deterrence. "The strategy of deterrence has assumed that this requirement of an ever triumphant will could be satisfied, if only because strength of will must somehow be proportionate to nobility of purpose. If our heart is pure, our hand will be steady, or at least steadier than

[28]Thomas C. Schelling: *The Strategy of Conflict*. Cambridge, Mass.: Harvard University Press, 1960, pp. 54, 57, 87.

the aggressor's." "To convince the adversary that we would act in the manner threatened, it is indispensable to convince ourselves that we would so respond. As long as we believe, others will believe. As long as others believe, they will not act. The key to a successful strategy of nuclear deterrence lies wholly within ourselves."[29] So, deterrence is a technical contrivance for doing what religion never could accomplish and the Christian religion never proposed (i.e., banish the *use* of force from human history), backed by an infinitude of correct anticipations of our anticipation of an enemy's anticipations, and so on.

The same American voluntarism is the source of our confidence in extreme "rationality of irrationality" policies, and it also has given birth to the thought that it is feasible and proper to fight a war of controlled countercity retaliation *as a bargaining tactic*. The question is not primarily whether cities can be deliberately exchanged with coolness and control enough to prevent this from at once becoming a spasm of countercity devastation. To this there is a prior question: whether exchanging cities for bargaining purposes and to play on the will of the adversary and break his resolve has not already transgressed the limits that are clearly present when war is understood as a trial of the actual military strength of nations. War as a test of the limitlessly variable "strength" of resolve may go as high as strategic city exchanges. War as a test of real strength to defend or effect objectives can and will go no higher than counterforces warfare. A nation determined to play a game of wills to the end, and resolved to will in accord with the internal "rationality" of a radical voluntarism, never will discover that there are any limits in resolutely willing to win this game of hostile wills in conflict. Not here is to be found any *ratio* in the *ultima ratio* of the arbitrament of arms. A nation comes upon no boundaries in this upward spiral, so long as proper acts of war are believed to arise not primarily out of concrete policy but out of contending wills. Unfortunately, in this, a commander can show his resolution in no other way than by proving he is willing to sacrifice one or more of his own cities; and he must reduce the enemy's cities to rubble as a means of getting at his resolution. This is the very definition of the unjust conduct of war.

Fighting a war has its obscure *ratio* only when the conduct of war is subordinated to the civil life and purposes of a nation, to its concrete civilization, values and policy objectives. The will to fight and the manner of fighting must be governed and controlled by the pre-eminence of society, and the effectuation or defense of its policy, over the use

[29]Robert W. Tucker: *The Just War: A Study of Contemporary American Doctrine.* Baltimore, Md.: The Johns Hopkins Press, 1960, p. 185.

of armaments. This relationship is lost sight of when war becomes a matter of one will "prevailing" over another, and the destruction of an entire city is made a mere means of "demonstrating" resolution, or is used to "symbolize" one side's willingness to go higher unless the other "chickens out."

Although analysts of the strategy of abstract conflict of wills would probably regard themselves as cool-headed rationalists in comparison with the warm-blooded "engagement" and passionate "involvement" recommended by contemporary existentialist philosophy, these schools are nevertheless brothers under the skin. The latter abstract from the structures of the person and the substance of inter-personal relationships and concentrate attention on only an *aspect* of the meeting of person with person, namely, the limitless capacity of self-consciousness to include in its consciousness the other's consciousness which in turn is determined only by its consciousness of the first person, and so on *ad infinitum.* Some existentialists reduce inter-personal relationships to a trial of wills or a test of resolution to "prevail," just as some analysts have pictured conflict between groups or nations. This is the secret meaning of the statement that countervalue warfare can, as a test of wills, have only *quantitative* limitations. This really means that there are no limits, except that quantity of destruction which will cause one side to give up first. If there had been more resolution to continue fighting (as there certainly might have been) the quantity would have been higher. No *ethical standards* are to be discovered for *inter-personal* behavior unless encounters between persons are imbedded in the nature of the persons and their good. No *political* limits are to be discovered for inter-national relations unless encounters between groups are imbedded in the structures of civil societies and their good. The wills and resolves of men must come down from aloft, they must return from their self-transcending "freedom" and limitless transcendence of the other in order to find that there are some things they are *bound not to do,* by the very nature of personhood, the very nature of political society, and the "natural justice" of warfare that is a purposive trial of strength with some controlling objective in view. The controlling goals in warfare may, of course, be "political effects objectives" which range far more widely than "battlefield objectives."[30] But surely, that contest is no longer "war" which has become a mere will to become demonstrably more resolute than someone else, by means that are not basically intended to insure that choiceworthy political effects will follow.

---

[30]Cf. Morton H. Halperin: *Limited War in the Nuclear Age.* Center of International Affairs, Harvard University, June, 1962, draft of an unpublished book.

War as a Limited Strategy

Analysts who now have managed to think this "unthinkable" thing
— limited counterpeople war — give evidence in what they say about
it that in this they have begun to think about the "un-do-able." It is
instructive that, in his recent book, Herman Kahn leans away from
Controlled City Reprisal toward Controlled Counterforce even more
than seemed to be the case in his first and major work, *On Thermonuclear War*.[31] He finds greater difficulty thinking about situations in
which an exchange of cities might seem justifiable in actual execution,
and (most significantly) he states with substance and at length the
political reason opposed to *doing* in this regard what he and other
analysts have *thought* with some exactitude while playing war games.
The same judgment — that controlled inter-city warfare is actually an
un-do-able plan of war — finds support also on almost every page of
the latest study specifically devoted to *Limited Strategic War*.[32] To be
sure, none of these analysts recommends such a war; they say only that
"limited strategic war is a *possible* war; to fight and prepare for such
a war is a possible strategy."[33] My contention, however, is that even
such a statement by a researcher goes too far, or not far enough toward
decision. It is a possible war and a possible strategy in the sense that
one can think of it after having not done so before: it is thinkable and
possible in this sense. But it is not a strategy that can be chosen and
put into effect by rational statesmanship, least of all by the government
of a free society.

---

[31]Princeton, N. J.: Princeton University Press, 1960.

[32]Edited by Klaus Knorr and Thornton Read. Published for the Center of International Studies, Princeton University, by Frederick A. Praeger, New York, 1962,
with chapters by each of the editors, and by Herman Kahn, Herbert D. Benington,
Morton A. Kaplan, Arthur Lee Burns, Clark C. Abt & Ithiel de Sola Pool, and
T. C. Schelling. My discussion of this volume of essays of necessity ignores significant differences among these authors.

[33]Knorr in Knorr and Read, *op. cit.*, pp. 5-6. "Limited strategic war" entails *long
range* exchanges; and this may mean (1) limited attacks on strategic *forces* or
(2) limited strategic attacks on *cities;* and the latter in turn may mean attacks
(a) on *evacuated* or (b) on *populated* cities. In commenting on a volume of
essays which analyses all these possible types of war under the heading of
"limited strategic war," I cannot avoid using the term "limited strategic war"
mainly to mean controlled counter-populated-city exchanges, which I deny is a
plan of war at all possible to be done. At the same time it should be clear that
I mean to allow that "limited strategic war," in the other senses, may possibly
be done and justly done. Certainly, limited attacks on strategic *forces* conforms
to the principles of *legitimate* military conduct. While unthinkable in one sense,
such a war is not un-do-able. One has to be more cautious, however, in describing
the conditions under which "countervalue" warfare that engages in exchanges of
cities allowed to be evacuated might be do-able, or could be a possibly legitimate
military action.

1. Limited nuclear attack on populated cities is only a limiting case of general nuclear war, and partakes of the same insanity. The fact is that weapons-analysts are only able to think of a war of controlled city exchanges as a *possibility for choice* by almost forcibly channelling their not inconsiderable intellectual powers in this direction, by resolutely concentrating their attention upon all-out general nuclear war as the *only* alternative to the one they are considering at the moment. This means that they first think of unlimited attack or unlimited retaliation, and then and by the aid of that unspeakable horror they manage to think of a limitation just short of that as possibly choiceworthy and do-able. Thus, Kahn writes: *"If the only alternatives are* between the all-out mutually homicidal war and the city exchange, bizarre and unpleasant as the city exchange is, it is not as bizarre and unpleasant as complete mutual homicide — even if a confusing and obsolete doctrine seems to make the latter the more conventional response. *It is precisely the value of this model that it jars me into adjusting intellectually* to the changed character of modern war."[34]

Klaus Knorr writes that limited strategic retaliation is "absolutely speaking, a calamity" so great that "a rational person will consider it only if all available alternatives are appreciably worse."[35] To be sure, he seems to believe that there may be a *number* of alternatives that might be worse; and he even implies that, if strategic forces become more stable and invulnerable, this *might* be a form of war frequently resorted to. I suggest, however, that this can be done, or genuinely considered only if the *sole* alternative is to go higher still, i.e., to go rapidly to all-out counter-city retaliation. This, at least, is what Knorr's conclusion seems to mean: "From every conceivable point of view it looks like a bad war and a bad strategy. But the question remains whether the available alternatives may not be, or may not come to be, more absurd and worse; and the possibility cannot be ruled out that *our* choices, *and* our opponent's choices, may become as absolutely bad as that implies."[36] It was probably the short distance between the greatest use and *this* "least undesirable" use of nuclear weapons that produced the first significant attempt to procure for this nation a wider range of choices: McNamara's move toward counterforces warfare. Significantly, in his concluding comment on these essays, T. C. Schelling

---

[34]*Thinking About the Unthinkable,* p. 134 (italics added). Or see p. 133: "The comparison should be made with the destructive all-out war, and the reader must fully understand that, *at least in our model,* this destruction really is total. Everybody is killed. Nobody is left. In these circumstances I believe one could expect the decision makers to prefer the controlled city exchange to the all-out war."

[35]Knorr and Read, *op. cit.,* p. 11.

[36]*Ibid.,* p. 30.

writes: "the concept of limited reprisal is something that a rational decision-maker can invent or discover in five minutes, once he is in a situation in which general war is an appalling prospect, a local tactical campaign is ineffectual, and inactivity and withdrawal are intolerable. It takes an act of intellect to *exclude* this kind of strategy from consideration. . . ."[37] It also takes an act of intellectual surrender to base strategy on city exchanges without making every effort to procure for ourselves other alternatives.

2. Whenever another pair of possible wars is in mind — when the analyst contrasts limited countervalue or countercity warfare with limited counterforces war — it seems very clear that the latter is choice-worthy for far more than quantitative reasons. Countercity or counter-people warfare is bizarre, whether it is limited or unlimited. Doubtless there are distinctions to be made according to whether such war (fought between commanders proving their resolve by means of their cities and people) is partially or totally destructive, whether one of the contending wills seeks to bargain and to prevail over the other in measured terms or goes all-out against that other will. There are distinctions of objective importance in comparative damage to the societies and in the number of casualties. But, in addition to these *quantitative* comparisons, there is also a *qualitative* distinction between countercity and counter-force which soon discloses itself in the midst of cool calculations of one-city-for-one or five-cities-for-one; and one cannot remain content with saying, "fifty cities is a lot to lose" nor contemplate for long actually *doing* the fighting of a war in which "Both A and B will run out of cities before B runs out of missiles."[38] So there are qualitative reasons to recommend that, as an upper limit, nuclear warfare limited to counter-force be designed, if there is to be nuclear war, and for as long as there remain any nuclear weapons.

3. The Knorr and Read volume reveals quite clearly the abyss of infinitude and illimitability into which strategic city exchange has already plunged. To this there are no real boundaries; and to speak of "quantitative" limitations is misleading and dangerous language. Even the understandings reached during the fighting will be arbitrary ones, maintained only by encounters of resolve. The bargaining is not only over survival or prevailing. It is also over "the criteria of behavior permissible in the nuclear age;"[39] such war is "a contest to define the rules of the game"[40] while the game is being played. The "teachers"

---

[37]*Ibid.*, p. 257.
[38]Cf. Kahn, *op. cit.*, pp. 138, 142.
[39]Kaplan in Knorr and Read, *op. cit.*, p. 149.
[40]*Ibid.*, p. 154.

must themselves be "learning" what they are going to will this war to be.[41] As Thornton Read puts it: if "strategic punishment is limited voluntarily," then it not only influences bargaining but is itself "also a subject to bargain about"; "when punishment is limited by the will (rather than the capability) to inflict it, every tactical engagement becomes an individual case of tacit bargaining."[42] An aspect of war that has always been present in it has now become its whole content: war now has to be "conducted according to rules that are themselves subject to tacit bargaining,"[43] for example, whether the cities exchanged are equivalent or accepted by the other side as an indication of equivalent or greater resolve. The expression Read uses, "a pure punitive contest," is itself probably too retrospective. This strategy is, on the contrary, primarily prospective: one side is teaching the other "strategic foresight." In contrast, punishment has an appositeness and may have limits, which are not to be found in war whose purpose is to convince your opponent that you have irreversibly passed (by slow motion, to be sure) to higher levels, because you are irrevocably committed to "appositeness *plus*" following each exchange. The side wins which first effectively communicates the fact that it will take two cities for one.

What then can Kaplan mean by saying that "limited strategic retaliation depends on and appeals to the inherent rationality of the players"? He means: "It induces them to think in cooperative rather than in strictly competitive ways. . . ."[44] But the writers of other essays make abundantly clear that this spiritualizing of conflict into cooperation only means "shared intimidation";[45] and only the optical illusion suffered by voluntarists and idealists can encourage one to imagine there must be more limits than in limited conventional war.[46] The more the players are lion-hearted and resolved to prevail, the more obvious it becomes that there are no boundaries to be found simply by pooling intimidation. On the contrary, each contestant must strive to demonstrate to the other that he is inexorably going higher. No matter how slow the pace up the scale of "value" exchanged, that side wins which appears most like an ascending force of nature. The "heart of the problem" for each contestant, once limited strategic retaliation has begun, is that he must "by individual examples . . . achieve the credibility of *an irreversible trend.*"[47]

---

[41]There are "probably intolerable 'expenses' of the educational program." Burns in Knorr and Read, *op. cit.*, p. 168.
[42]*Ibid.*, pp. 82, 84, 86.
[43]*Ibid.*, pp. 82, 84, 86.
[44]*Ibid.*, p. 158.
[45]Knorr and Schelling in Knorr and Read, pp. 21 and 247.
[46]Kaplan in Knorr and Read, p. 159.
[47]Abt and de Sola Pool in Knorr and Read, pp. 220-21 (italics added).

The way to win such a war is to get in the car, cold sober, with 20-20 vision and with the steering mechanism in perfect working condition, but with an accelerator so contrived that it will press itself very, very slowly to the floor unless and until the car's radar picks up a beam which tells it that the other car has pulled off the road or that its driver has retarded its speed. T. C. Schelling's comment at the end of this volume is worth noting, concerning a "mistake that one can be seduced into," and, he seems to imply, one made by some of the contributors. This is the supposition that "to conduct war in the measured cadence of limited reprisal somehow . . . gives it rational qualities that it would otherwise lack." Instead, writes Schelling:

> The situation is fundamentally indeterminate as far as logic goes. There is no logical reason why two adversaries will not bleed each other to death, drop by drop, each continually feeling that if he can only hold out a little longer, the other is bound to give in. There is no assurance that both sides will not come to feel that everything is at stake in this critical test of endurance, that to yield is to acknowledge unconditional submissiveness.

It is cold comfort that the foregoing statement is preceded by the sentence: "Even if this kind of warfare were irrational, it could still enjoy the benefits of slowness, of deliberateness, and of self-control"[48] — except that here Schelling inadvertently makes backhanded reference to another kind of rationality in the conduct of war than the "rationality of irrationality." A slow lobbing value-for-value war, like deterrence by threat of massive retaliation, can best be conducted by providing in advance for making an increasingly "choiceless choice."[49] This can be done, at the time and in the increasingly un-do-able fashion it has to be done, only by "making" oneself actually or apparently less and less the doer of it.

4. The fact that controlled city exchanges are an "un-do-able" way to conduct war becomes evident in the fact that Kahn can think this "unthinkable" only by thinking of its being done *once*. "It is, in fact, hard to imagine a 'controlled' city exchange or similar limited Countervalue attack being used more than once in two generations," he writes. "If used once, the shock might be sufficient to cause drastic and irreversible changes in the international order that would make repetitions unlikely."[50] He lists the objections against limited general war in order of increasing importance, and places last the objection that "surely

---

[48]Knorr and Read, *op. cit.*, p. 255. Also see Knorr, p. 5: "Only in a crudely descriptive and arbitrary sense would it be possible to say where limited strategic war ends and 'unlimited' general war begins."

[49]Cf. Benington in Knorr and Read, *op. cit.*, p. 123.

[50]Cf. Kahn, *op. cit.*, p. 63.

even if it worked once or twice it will eventually escalate into all-out war, and that would be the end."[51] Whereupon Kahn comes down heavily on the side of this objection:

> It is, in fact, inconceivable to me that such a system could continue. The objection is less to the strategy than to the model of two nation states both armed to the teeth, both regularly playing a version of the juvenile game of chicken, and yet both somehow expecting the system to last for a long time. I do not believe that this is possible. The proper, possibly the only, way to view this type of controlled war is as an attempt to use what influence one has, while one has it, to "vote" on the system which replaces our current deterrent system with its negotiation and resolution of disputes and political objectives against a background of threatened mutual homicide. One possible effect of a controlled exchange might be a heightened sense of crisis and danger plus a greater realization of the two nations' mutual interest in developing a better system — this could end in a détente.[52]

Surely this says as plainly as anything can that Controlled Nuclear Reprisals against cities is not a proper form of war at all. Into this none of the definite objectives of a nation are extensible at the time of the action. The scenario describes a critical *transition* from City Reprisals to purposive action. In itself, it cannot be politically *done*. If it is thinkable as being done once only before another line of action takes its place, and if city exchanges cannot even be done once with the expectation that the system is going to last for a long time, then the task of statesmanship is to think through such a critical transition without engaging in it and to initiate action that can continue, if need be, in behalf of definite policies.

If what Kahn supposes is what happens, let this not be called a plan of war among others that can be drawn up. It is rather a catastrophe that exceeds all the limits of warfare, for the purpose of teaching ourselves, and the world, a lesson that might have been otherwise learned simply by taking a little thought *within* the limits war now has, as a just barely purposive extension of politics. For the scenario which begins "the morning after" city exchanges is as follows:

> . . . the President of the United States might send a copy of this book [Granville Clark and Louis B. Sohn, *World Peace Through World Law*, Cambridge, Mass.: Harvard University Press, 1958] to Premier Khru-

---

[51]*Ibid.*, p. 133. Some contributors to the Knorr and Read volume seem to believe that limited strategic war may frequently be used in an era of balanced and invulnerable missile bases. But those who suggest this are using the term "strategic war" to mean strategic counterforces warfare. Thus Morton Kaplan writes that he "tends to believe that, *unless limited strategic nuclear war reaches the city-busting stage*, it can probably be used at least several times." (Knorr and Read, *op. cit.*, p. 161, italics added.)

[52]*Ibid.*, p. 135.

shchev, saying, "There's no point in your reading this book; you will not like it any more than I did. I merely suggest you sign it, right after my signature. This is the only plan that has been even roughly thought through; let us therefore accept it. We surely do not wish to set up a commission to study other methods of organizing the world, because within weeks both of us will be trying to exploit our common danger for unilateral advantages. If we are to have a settlement, we must have it now, before the dead are buried."[53]

Instead of even once doing the unthinkable which is "un-do-able," it might even be possible to think in another (habitually) unthinkable direction: "serious, tough-minded study of world government or other 'alternatives' might even result in a scheme's being devised that could be negotiated without the pressure of war,"[54] or rather without contriving a catastrophe illegitimately called "war" to "make" ourselves think politically. In any case, it is significant that most of the viable war plans Kahn runs through in his recent volume (in settings that are more imaginable in real political encounters than the *one* model that can ever give countercity reprisals an apparent choice-worthiness) are controlled counterforce, or this *plus avoidance* of civilian damage, even when this seems to sacrifice some military advantage!

5. Finally, there are internal considerations, as well as external ones, why even limited city exchanges must be judged politically un-do-able, especially by the government of a free society, un-do-able even once in the expectation that such a system will continue:

> If every time a hard decision has to be made, a major portion of the country has to be risked; if every time a country's diplomat walks into a hostile conference room, every man, woman and child feels threatened; if every time a nation stands firm against aggressive probes, panic seizes the hearts of many of its citizens, then many citizens will simply adopt an attitude of denial or apathetic fatalism. Others will call for "peace" at any price with such intensity that their governments will have to get out of their way. There may even be some who will say, "Better a fearful end than endless fear." Responsible political life is likely to suffer disastrously as a result of a combination of apathy, denial, and hysteria. The trouble with "negotiating" in this atmosphere is that, to put it mildly, it is not likely to produce thoughtful, considered suggestions or programs. It will instead invite blackmail and deception by the government which is in better control of its people, and irresponsible rigidity or destabilizing weakness by the government which cannot manipulate its people.[55]

This says as plainly as anything can that war-plans based on the premise that civilian lives and property are to be sacrificed indiscrim-

---

[53]*Ibid.*, p. 148.
[54]*Ibid.*, p. 150.
[55]*Ibid.*, pp. 214-15.

inately or made the object of attack in planned city exchanges, however controlled, are imaginable only in a world in which legitimate political activity has already been strangled. Men, cities, and politics have already been put to death, in thinking this unthinkable thing that is also, in and of its very nature, politically "un-do-able" conduct in war. This is not a surprising conclusion, since the "natural justice" of counterforces warfare defines the upper limit of the use of force which is politically justifiable.

To this reader, the most interesting chapter in the Knorr and Read volume is that by Clark C. Abt and Ithiel de Sola Pool on "The Constraint of Public Attitudes." This is an inquiry into whether the strategy under consideration can "satisfy the constraints of the politically possible."[56] This, happily, is "not, in any rigorous sense, a researchable subject,"[57] except by means of speculative scenarios. The response of people, and particularly of a people who have a measure of influence on their government's decisions, to city exchanges is in no sense comparable to their reaction to the destruction of an entire town by a natural disaster, nor even to their probable reaction to damage of the same magnitude that may be the unavoidable side-effect of counterforces nuclear war. To speculate about what their reaction will be is, I believe, to speculate about the rudiments of the "just war doctrine" that still makes its presence felt.

The most these authors seem able to say in behalf of a countercity war-plan is that "the strategy may still be worth planning for if it can be a contingency policy, available for use if public opinion turns out to tolerate it. . . .[58] Even the idea of folding this war away in a contingency plan is not actually supported by their findings of probable fact. It is true that during the time of actual execution one possible public reaction counterbalances another. Perhaps the people in threatened cities "would channel their fears and anxieties into the direct self-protective actions of evacuation rather than into civil protest."[59] Perhaps, on the other hand, "substantial portions of the people living in the cities threatened with prompt counter-reprisals, *if given time to make their opinions known on the matter*, would be violently opposed to the United States' initiation of limited reprisal against Novosibirsk."[60]

The question, however, concerns civil protest not only during the execution of this strategy, but also *before, during,* and *afterward,* unless

---

[56]Knorr and Read, *op. cit.,* p. 199.
[57]Knorr in Knorr and Read, *op. cit.,* p. 23.
[58]*Op. cit.,* p. 204.
[59]*Ibid.,* p. 215.
[60]*Ibid.,* p. 214.

politics has already been put to death before cities and people are. Statesmen cannot long remain, if they ever are, isolated from the civil life it is their function to serve. Therefore, "the major inhibition felt by the President would be his *perception* of what public opinion was likely to be *after* the crisis." To be prepared to fight a counterforces war requires a "community" fall-out shelter system, correlated with private shelters. To be prepared to fight a countercity war, however, would make it rather dangerous for the statesman to allow the people thus to congregate, since "large communal shelters in cities might be the scene of considerable political agitation that might have both immediate and long-term effects."[61] People must be isolated from one another if a decision-maker is to be sufficiently isolated from them to make this a do-able policy. Free political life would have to be put to death if this is the way a nation's survival is to be engineered. This analysis is revelatory of the inherently non-political character of this supposed strategy. It means that "many of the problems that may result from the adoption of a policy of limited retaliation could arise if the policy were even considered with sufficient seriousness for people to believe that it might be undertaken."[62]

So there they stand, these "spiritualized" conquerors, each seeking to "prevail" by throwing cities to rubble, as wealthy dandies in San Francisco used to fight their "duels" by throwing gold dollars into the Bay until one of them had the will to do so no longer. It is evident that the people of one of the selected cities will have to be put out of politics before they can knowingly agree to their own government's arbitrary resolve to use them in this game of tit-for-tat. And it would be *their own* government's resolve and not that of the enemy alone, since if this game stays limited everything will depend on the enemy's attacking no more cities or cities only a little larger than those we have "signaled" him to take out by our own immediately prior choice of targets from among his cities. This is a war that is supposed to be fought slowly up the range of the "value" we and the enemy have agreed to place on cities in order that the sacrifice of them will, in turn, effectively signal the enemy our determination to go somewhat higher than he.

So there they stand, these "spiritual" warriors, as they engage in a war of nerves, each saying to the other, "There, you see, one of us

[61]*Ibid.*, p. 215.

[62]*Ibid.*, p. 237. Under this strategy, the relation of the people of our cities to their government domestically is the same as the relation of a smaller ally to an alliance thinking of adopting this policy, if the ally is apt to be offered as target or more of a target. See, in Knorr and Read, Arthur Lee Burns on "The Problem of Alliances."

has to be rational, and since it's not going to be me, it has to be you, or you first." This war of "value for value"

> can be regarded as a late and perhaps last desperate move in the *economization* of war and world politics. Arms and men are more or less scarce means having alternative uses; resources such as cities, fertile countrysides, and even stable social systems are in one aspect, economic goods—as implied in the strategic term countervalue. [63]

The people of a country cannot knowingly accept their complete inclusion in this process of the *economization* of politics by which they themselves are reduced to the status of values in exchange. No government responsive to their will or responsible for their weal can conduct war in this fashion. In contrast, the civil damage collateral to actually fighting a counterforces war will seem rationally directed to some purpose, and is intended to be, even if the damage proves as extensive or more. As with massive or balanced deterrence, so with value-for-value war that has none but the quantitative limits which the weakness of one side's resolve may allow: these war-plans are intrinsically intolerable. Both are tolerated only because people don't think about them or because people who think about them stand several steps back from thinking through the actual doing of them, or because they think grimly that, if only we have these wars in preparation and are strong enough in our will to use them, why, then none of them will ever have to be used.

On the other hand, no one should blink the fact that the transformation of "political man" into "economic man" may have proceeded so far in the contemporary period that it has become an irreversible trend in this civilization. Then modern man will sooner or later destroy himself. This will be because of his merely quantitative evaluation of human life and of ethical and political conduct, because of the economization of politics, and his lack of capacity for political agency and for making sound political judgments concerning the do-able and the inherently un-do-able. These things increasingly characterize all of the realms of decision. This leads, in international relations, to a nation's unquestioning acceptance of the supposed rationality of countervalue warfare.

Suggested Policy Decisions

The "just conduct" of war proscribing deliberate direct attack upon non-combatants, and the primacy in war of weapon-to-weapon

---

[63] Burns in Knorr and Read, *op. cit.*, p. 170.

trials of strength over a contest of wills, are not of course immediately *constitutive* of policy decisions or war plans. But these are *regulative* of such decisions, so long as war remains in any measure a definite purposive political act.

I will venture here to suggest a series of policy decisions which seem to me imperative at this hour for the free world's security. These suggestions are put forward with a great degree of reluctance, since I do not believe that ethico-political analysis extends so far beyond providing regulative moral guidance. Not every decision, not even every important decision, is an *ethical* decision, and many exceedingly important choices are the business of statesmen and of experts other than the moralist. Still, with the aid of other experts the following suggestions can be made for steps that need urgently to be taken. None of these decisions waits on international agreement. Each must be *declared* policy, and each can at least begin to be put into effect by "unilateral initiatives."

1. This nation, and other nations of the West, need increasingly to procure forces for sub-conventional and conventional warfare, and at the same time to repair in public consciousness a doctrine of the possible and just use of such forces. Of course, it may be said about conventional forces that we lost that "arms race" with the Russians long ago, or rather never sought seriously to enter upon it. It is also true that the strength needed for conventional warfare would require a change of heart in that "economic man" who bears the name of the free world taxpayer. He must be told in no uncertain terms that his unexamined reliance on deterrence of total war by threat of total war and mutual homicide policies are themselves of a piece with his unwillingness to prepare for any real trial of strength. He must be told that he is in mortal danger precisely because at every level of warfare he is so completely non-political and unpurposive. Hoping to banish the use of force by threatening unusable force, he only banishes usable force and pulls the nerve of action. It is an ominous weakness in the West that the enemy can heat a crisis to almost any temperature knowing that the West will be no better prepared after the event. Men will be called up, it is true, but we now give a crisis-maker the luxury of knowing in advance that very soon the *status quo ante* will be restored.[64] The free world taxpayer must be awakened from the dream of deterrence; and he must be told that we cannot make unjust, inter-city warfare measur-

---

[64] On the same pleasant summer evening in August 1962, the "Seven O'Clock Report" showed film and the voices of reservists complaining how useless their call-up was ten months ago, and a commentator's analysis of the evidences that Russian military might was being mobilized in support of another Berlin crisis about to be created.

ably more of an impossibility without making just or counterforces war-fare again a possibility. This means, first and foremost, strength in conventional arms; and there is no analyst who does not say that NATO could match the mythical Russian "hordes," and the whole free world could do this at every point of probable vital challenge.

If religious opinion has any influence on public opinion, and that in turn on high-level policy decisions, then a false Christian identification of the peace of God with the peace of the earthly city must bear a share of responsibility for this nation's reliance on war that can never under any circumstances be fought, and its simultaneous abandonment of the sort of war that can be used. No churchman can condemn the one without condemning the other. He cannot in good conscience oppose the present reliance of the U.S. on massive weapons unless he also confesses that, during the period we developed this reliance, a general "Christian" pacifism contributed to it and to our present design of war by a sweeping opposition to a more equitable and universal military service. In 1948, for example, it required only a one or two-man social action lobby of the Presbyterian church and a few telephone calls to prominent Presbyterians in Oklahoma to determine the vote of one representative which was decisive in Republican caucus in bottling up a universal training bill in committee and in insuring that it never reached the floor of Congress for debate.[65]

2. This nation should announce that as a matter of policy we will never be the first to use nuclear weapons—*except* tactical ones that may and will be used, against forces only and not strategically against an enemy's heartland, to stop an invasion across a clearly defined boundary, our own or one we are pledged by treaty to defend. This would make it unambiguously clear that tactical nuclear weapons will be used if need be against any invasion, even by conventional forces. The threat would be believable, because of the clearly declared limits which state that the use of nuclear weapons will be defensive only and that not even in reply to an invasion will we first use nuclear weapons

---

[65]See R. Morton Darrow, "The Church and Techniques of Political Action" in *Religion in American Life*, ed. by J. W. Smith and Leland Jamison. Princeton, N. J.: Princeton University Press, 1960, Vol. II, pp. 186-7. The author considers only the technique of making religious opinion politically effective, not the substance of the matter.

After a nuclear war, the survivors may well ask concerning the complicity of the churches and "peace" groups in the assistance our government gave to the enemy in killing people he did not want to kill—by locating missiles near populated cities and by failing to construct a national system of community fall-out shelters. If this question is asked, the answer can only be that such resulted from the effort good people of the previous age made never to grow accustomed to the idea of nuclear war, from their resolve instead to avoid war altogether, and from the natural kinship between their views and *pacifistic deterrence*.

"offensively" against an enemy's territory or his strategic forces. This would make it unnecessary for the President of the United States constantly to warn off a possible invasion of Europe by words that allow the possibility of our initiating the use of nuclear weapons, and possibly an offensive strike against Russian cities or against her strategic bases. This proposal may be called the right of first defensive use of nuclear weapons against invading forces, or a commitment to use nuclear weapons first only over one's own territory.

This proposal has been made by Paul Nitze,[66] and more recently by Leo Szilard[67] and Thornton Read.[68] While Szilard's formulation should be looked at to see the significance of the inclusion of this policy decision among the tenets of a Council for Abolishing War, the fuller and sounder analysis by Thornton Read affords us the clearest way to elaborate further the meaning of this second policy proposal. Thornton Read has written most eloquently and forcefully concerning the value of preserving the distinction between conventional and nuclear weapons as such, of preserving the fear the people of the world have of ever again crossing this boundary, and of channelling this fear into a proposal for neutralizing nuclear weapons in a system of international sanctions against their use.[69] Without even invoking the danger of escalating from tactical to massive nuclear weapons, he has satisfactorily demonstrated the essentially escalatory character of tactical nuclear weapons themselves, because of the relation of their weight to their fire power in comparison with conventional explosives, a relation which places a great gulf between conventional and tactical nuclears as possible instruments of controlled warfare.[70]

Thornton Read does not lightly find virtue in a proposal involving a possible first use of tactical nuclears. The fact is that he can do so only because he thinks it may be possible to link legitimate first use of tactical nuclears with another well-understood limit, namely, national boundaries, which may serve as a focus of agreement concerning the rules of conflict. This is his proposal for defensive first use in or over one's own invaded territory. Such a declaration of policy is, of course, a positive assertion of legitimacy which requires, and makes it possible

---

[66]*East-West Negotiations.* Washington Center of Foreign Policy Research, 1958, pp. 28-36.

[67]"Are We On The Road to War?" *Bulletin of the Atomic Scientists,* April, 1962.

[68]"The Proposal to Use Nuclear Weapons Over One's Own Territory," Unpublished paper, Center of International Studies, Princeton, 1962.

[69]*A Proposal to Neutralize Nuclear Weapons.* Center of International Studies, Princeton. Policy Memorandum No. 22, Dec. 15, 1960.

[70]"Counterforce Strategies and Arms Control," Center of International Studies, Princeton, March, 1962 (unpublished); and Knorr and Read, *op. cit.,* pp. 72-77.

to declare, that not even to stop a massive conventional invasion will we use nuclear weapons offensively first. *This possibility we now hold ambiguously open* for ourselves, in order to "strengthen the deterrent." Yet in view of the destruction an offensive first strike over an enemy's territory would immediately let loose over own own, it has become increasingly unbelievable we will ever employ it for any of the definite military or political objectives involved in recent crises. Thus, the proposal is that we publicly renounce that first use of nuclear weapons which we can really mean to renounce, while asserting a defensive first use of tactical nuclears tied to the repulsion of an invasion across a conventionally defended boundary.

> National boundaries have the same sort of clarity and symbolic significance as the distinction between conventional and nuclear weapons. Crossing the nuclear threshold has, in fact, been compared to crossing a national boundary. Both limits are unambiguous and both are the focus for strong feelings.
>
> The proposal to use nuclear weapons defensively combines two sharp and unambiguous discontinuities in the spectrum of violence and says that crossing a clear-cut geographical boundary justifies the opponent in crossing the equally clear-cut discontinuity between conventional and nuclear weapons.[71]

It may also be added that the qualitative discontinuity between counterforce and counterpeople warfare is tied in with boundaries, if nuclear weapons are ever justifiably used. The side using nuclear weapons justifiably would have every incentive to limit their destructiveness, and to maintain sufficient conventional forces either to hold the border or to slow an invasion so that civilians could be evacuated from between the lines. Moreover, "the region that is fair game for a nuclear attack is not only clearly defined and small in area; *it does not even exist until the aggressor creates it.*" The objective in this use of tactical nuclears will not be "victory" but defense strictly understood as sealing the border. "At the border there would be a discontinuity in the life expectancy of enemy soldiers. In crossing the border residual life expectancy would drop from, say, fifty years to fifty minutes. This would establish a powerful incentive not to cross and would create serious problems of morale for the aggressor."

This is certainly a clear case of "just conduct" in a first resort to nuclear weapons. It is counterforces warfare, surrounded by the additional limitation of the aggressor-defender distinction. And it allows "bargaining" and an encounter of wills in which rules of warfare may

---

[71]Thornton Read, "The Proposal to Use Nuclear Weapons Over One's Own Territory" (Unpublished). Subsequent undesignated quotations are also from this document.

be agreed to, created, preserved or enforced. Here the aim is not "to bind a potential violator through his sense of honor" but "to influence his behavior by creating in his mind expectations as to how we will respond." This is its superiority over a simple proscription of aggression.

At the same time, in contrast to our present policy which admits the possibility of a first initiation of nuclear warfare over his territory, "the advantage of the more restrictive rule is that it is more credible" and therefore more likely to deter, more likely to bring about tacit agreements to limit nuclear war and to restrict it to forces. The point is to "emphasize the distinction between the defensive and the offensive use of nuclear weapons so that it becomes a focus of expectations comparable to the nuclear-conventional distinction." Breaching the latter distinction may serve to enforce the former. This proposal is, therefore, also a struggle over the rules of warfare. "An aggressor having superior conventional forces would try to establish the rule that nuclear weapons should not be used at all. The defender would want to establish the rule that nuclear weapons could be used defensively but not offensively." But this is far removed from a limitless struggle of empty wills, each only reflecting the other.

Before going on to my third point, a comment may be inserted here concerning Leo Szilard's formulation of this proposal that "*America could and should adopt the policy that, in case of war, if she were to use atomic bombs against troops in combat, she would do so only on her own side of the prewar boundary.*"[72] Against the objection that it is an odd war, indeed, in which weapons with the greater destructive side-effects are reserved for use over one's own territory, Szilard gives the obvious answer: "I do not know to what extent West German cities could be spared by a judicious tactical use of atomic bombs by American forces, but I do know that if America were to use bombs beyond the pre-war boundary, West German cities would be destroyed by Russian bombs." In comparison with "the simple pledge renouncing the use of the bomb" altogether, the proposed commitment "would be easier to keep and therefore it would be a more believable pledge" (though Szilard does suggest that "it would be possible for Western Europe to build up within five years conventional forces to the point where it could renounce the use of atomic bombs against troops in combat in case of war").

To announce unilaterally, as Szilard proposes, this limitation upon any first use of nuclears requires us also to renounce unilaterally "*plans which call for a first strike against Russian rocket and strategic bases*

---

[72]*Op. cit.*

35

in case of war" and to renounce *"the policy of 'deterring' Russia, with the threat that America would resort to such a first strike in case of war."* The "general *deterrent"* would be given up; and in urging this surely Szilard is correct when he says that America would not "lose much by giving up the threat of strategic bombing because the deterrent effect of such a threat is negligible unless the threat is believable," which increasingly it is not. A *second* strike, however, should be maintained, as a threat and a promise, in case *"American cities or bases are attacked with bombs, or if there is an unprovoked attack with bombs against one of America's allies."* Szilard's use of the word "bomb" for all nuclears is inexact, of course. He probably means to justify an attack first upon the strategic *forces* of an enemy who has used tactical nuclears offensively on the territory of our allies. If so, the above statement amounts to a crucial point yet to be considered in Read's rule for restricting legitimate use of nuclears to one's own territory, namely, that any violation of this rule will, for the first time, make offensive strikes legitimate over the enemy's territory. Szilard's present proposal shows that when a powerful intellect (even though his mind is the mind of a scientist) focuses attention on the grave problem of war today, he will be driven to follow the lineaments of the just war doctrine in his policy proposals.[73] Something like this is what anyone will come up with if he focuses attention on how we are to "back away from the war to which we have come dangerously close," and to which we still stand too dangerously close.

---

[73]Szilard's mind wanders from the problem of concrete political and military policy, and his political objectives "which must be pursued in the next couple of years" turn into "steps" which must be taken toward a more lofty goal, and are of value only if they lead to this goal. These policy proposals, which surely are worthwhile in themselves to limit war, are only "in order to make the present danger of war recede to the point where attention could be focused on the task of abolishing war."

No one would deny that attention must be given to this task, but it must be political reason and political action which attend to it. Unfortunately, in Szilard's case, it is "scientific" reason instead of the political reason he exercised in the concrete proposals. These are all set in the context of the formation of a "Council for Abolishing War." This Council is to have "fellows (who are all scientists)" and would elect a board of directors, on which "membership would not be restricted to scientists." A panel of political advisors, of course, would be assembled. The scientific Council would by these means formulate two sets of objectives. "To the first set belong those objectives which can not be attained at the present time through political action because it would take further inquiry, and perhaps even real research to know, in concrete terms, what needs to be done. To the second set belong those objectives which can be pursued through political action because it is clear what needs to be done [presumably Szilard's concrete policy proposals]." A *political* movement will be brought into being to enable us to back away "from purposeless warfare. *Scientific* research may then tell us how to abolish it altogether." Thus, "the combination of a few per cent of the votes and the sweet voice of reason might turn out to be an effective combination."

3. In the foregoing, we have bracketed for the moment the question whether the first use of tactical nuclears only between the front line and the border crossed is a rule we want simply for the five years needed to mount adequate conventional forces, or whether this self-imposed rule of war should be regarded as a permanent part of justifiable resistance to conventional invasion in a nuclear age. Should the United States have as its ultimate goal the preparation of conventional defense so that as soon as possible it can accept a prohibition of *any* first use of nuclear weapons?

73(*Continued*)

A conversation between Szilard and Polanyi is not, I think, untypical of this sort of reasoning. Polanyi said that, since it might be suicidal for people to be *overly* generous, "perhaps the rule ought to be 'Be one per cent more generous to people than they are to you.' This should be sufficient . . . because if everyone were to follow this rule, the earth would, step by step, turn into a livable place." [An alternative name for Szilard's Council is "Council for a Livable World."] To which in reply Szilard summed up the phenomena in human nature and politics which theologians have always called the boundless "sin" of man, by saying, "each is bound to think that he is 30 per cent more generous than the other;" and he proceeded to slay this with a rule: "Perhaps if we were to stipulate as the rule of conduct 'Be 31 per cent more generous to others than they are to you' such a rule might work." Everywhere in this article Szilard describes the men he wants in his proposed Council and movement as men who have an adequate "historical" point of view, meaning (I think) men who believe the bomb has completely changed the nature of history and of politics; and who are as a consequence resolved to reconcile the nations by rules and abolish war by additional research in the time provided by concrete political proposals. This is exceedingly *un*historical and *non*-political reasoning.

This may seem needlessly harsh on that great man and generous spirit who is Leo Szilard. I have already paid tribute to his concrete proposals as disclosing the very anatomy of just and rational conduct in war. But one cannot forget the fact that Szilard was also the first to propose that *countervalue* warfare be planned and, if need be, put into execution. ("Disarmament and the Problem of Peace," *Bulletin of the Atomic Scientists,* October 1955, pp. 297-307.) Once he also speculatively proposed a variant of Kahn's Doomsday deterrent machine: cadres of Russian demolition experts under New York City and an American demolition team under Moscow, to make certain neither side can ever fire their massive weapons because neither *can* want to, and because both are now *bound* to want peace. ("The Mined Cities," *Bulletin of the Atomic Scientists,* Dec. 1961, pp. 407-412.) To such proposals the ascendency of the scientific mind in politics almost invariably comes. (For an excellent study of scientific advisors in government, the undeniable political character of their "scientific" advice, and the additional confusion introduced by the fact that they often fail to acknowledge this, see Robert Gilpin: *American Scientists and Nuclear Weapons Policy.* Princeton, N. J.: Princeton University Press, 1962.) Such proposals are in play because of the ascendency of "making" over principles for the guidance of political agency and inherent in proper "doing." One must question, not the present proposals themselves, but whether they are soundly grounded. Is not Szilard and the "scientific" mind generally just a special case of the modern mentality which out of limitless passion for peace on earth might be willing to design and do unlimited war? Was it because he simply became convinced his former proposals could not be "made" to work or because he began to think politically that Szilard wrote his recent article? Does *he* understand that his concrete proposals were born out of the morality of war's conduct which has validity in a multi-national world long before and apart from the descent of peace?

37

The more one thinks about a policy of using tactical nuclears defensively, and unilateral initiatives to try to govern war in this fashion, the more it seems a possible choice for the nations of the world. At least they would be forced to ask whether it is only for the time being that security for the free world and the peace of the entire world could be based on this proposal. If this first use of nuclear arms can be tied to the resistance of aggression across well-understood and conventionally well-defended boundaries, will not free world security and world peace be less in danger? Will not this be better than an absolute distinction between conventional and nuclear explosives as a basis for the peace-keeping machinery of some future international organization? Or, on the contrary, ought we to begin now to strengthen conventional forces with a view to placing all nuclear weapons in a class by themselves as illegitimate weapons (like bacteriological weapons) which may be possessed to deter their use by an enemy but never used first even in self-defense?[74]

In whichever way this question is decided, it is of great importance that freedom-loving and peace-loving people realize that to renounce the first use of any weapon is a matter more of what they do than of what they say. "To the extent that the Communists are unable to defeat the conventional forces of the free world without resorting to nuclear weapons, the practical effect will be our renunciation of the first use of nuclear weapons."[75] This means that at the moment we may have simply presented the Russians with the ability effectively to renounce the first use of tactical nuclears in the European theater.

4. Nuclear capability must be maintained for use in counterforce strikes over an enemy's territory. These strikes would have a dual purpose: first, to prosecute the trial of strength and destroy or decrease an enemy's forces and the force he can muster on the battlefield; secondly, to punish any violation and thus to enforce if possible the rule which we declare by word and by action we have imposed on ourselves, namely, that while defensive first use of tactical nuclear weapons is legitimate, not even in answer to this will we tolerate the use of tactical nuclear weapons offensively over the territory of another nation. Both these purposes indicate that nuclear weapons over an enemy's territory should first be used against *tactical* objectives, munitions dumps, supply lines, bridges, etc. If *nuclear* weapons are used to do this, their

---

[74]There is an excellent summary of the arguments for eliminating *any* first use of even tactical nuclear weapons from Western military policy in Halperin, *op. cit.* He, however, does not explicitly consider the possibility of tying first use to a self-imposed and announced policy limiting the use of nuclear weapons to one's own invaded territory.

[75]Henry Kissinger, *The Necessity for Choice.* New York: Harper, 1960, p. 91.

use will both prosecute the war and be a signal that the right to do this was granted when the enemy first used nuclear power offensively across another nation's boundary. The reasons for the limitation of these retaliatory strikes to tactical targets, however, will have to be declared again and again and communicated to both the enemy and neutral nations.

If *tactical* targets are clearly the objectives of an answering offensive use of nuclear weapons, the distinction Thornton Read makes between these two uses may be a little too severe:

> The defensive use is primarily to act on the opponent's capability, to deny him territory. The offensive use is rather to act on his will, to punish him and to communicate to him our resolve and our determination not only to defend our territory but to uphold the two rules he has violated, namely the rule against conventional aggression and the rule against the use (or first use) of nuclear weapons against another nation's territory.[76]

Acting upon his will is, of course, important, perhaps now of added importance, but one is still engaged in war to deny him territory and cause him to withdraw. Moreover, in acting upon his will one is doing so by just and limited counterforce means, and with the objective of achieving possible political effects in societies that may endure beyond the conflict.

5. We come now to the No City strategy discussed in the first parts of this paper. The statement of U.S. policy that McNamara presented in his University of Michigan address, if carried out, would place as wide a "firebreak" as possible between a war of exchanges involving strategic forces and counter-city strategic warfare. There should also be a "firebreak" between conventional and tactical nuclear warfare—by, for example, not equipping the same troops with both types of weapons—and another between strikes against tactical targets and strikes against strategic forces.

We ought not to say at once that, in the nuclear age, "a main consequence of limited war, and a main purpose for engaging in it, is *to raise the risk of general war.*"[77] Since "general war" ambiguously embraces both attacks on an enemy's strategic forces and attacks upon his cities, this implies that a main purpose of engaging in any form of limited war is to indicate that we are prepared to go to massive retaliation against cities. This is to regard the main purpose of any of the forms of limited war as a simple trial of wills. We ought rather to say that one of the consequences and one of the purposes of limited con-

---

[76]*Op. cit.,* p. 29.
[77]T. C. Schelling, "Nuclear Strategy in Europe," *World Politics,* Vol. XIV, No. 3 (April, 1962), p. 421.

ventional or tactical nuclear war is *to raise the risk of counterforce strategic war.* A nation which first makes use of tactical nuclear weapons to resist a conventional aggression, for example, says by that action that it may be finally willing to use strikes against the enemy's homeland tactical targets or missile bases to impose on him its self-imposed rule that nuclear weapons are to be used only defensively and to punish any violation of this limit. The latter is clearly one purpose of nuclear war at the first level. Its main purpose is to seal the border and defend the country. Its main purpose, in any case, is not to raise the risk but to preserve a limit.

Moreover, the risk which the defender raises is still counterforces warfare and not the mutual destruction of societies. The will to fight "counterforce plus avoidance" can be signalled to the enemy, can work to keep war limited and enforce tacit or declared agreements about the rules of war in international law, *only* if one is able to fight such a war marked off as clearly as possible from "general war." One must have the ability to carry limited counterforce warfare to the enemy's own territory in order to bargain effectively about the limits and rules by which war is to be fought.

6. Just as it would be wrong to say of unconventional, conventional, or tactical nuclear war that it is *nothing but* deterrence during the war, so it is also wrong to say that a No City Strategy "is nothing but deterrence during a war." Counterforce strikes over an enemy's territory, and preparations to limit war to this, do replace the assumption of massive general deterrence policy (so far as it is possible to deter a rational enemy *before* the war starts) with the assumption that "it surely is possible to deter that rational enemy from going to city destruction even if the war starts."[78] Such deterrence during strategic strikes against forces is only an aspect of even this war, whose principal purpose is to enforce *lower* limits, punish violations of them, and in any case decrease the enemy's military capability and affect the balance of power in the world after the war is over.

Still, all forms of limited war, including counterforce strikes over the enemy's territory, do have this additional purpose of reducing his will to fight, or to fight in certain ways, by indicating our possible willingness to go higher still. The capstone of this system, which includes war at any of the lower limits in a nuclear age, is finally the deterrence of city destruction by the threat of city destruction. Thus, Fryklund sums up the No City Strategy that may now be in the making:

---

[78]Richard Fryklund, *op. cit.,* p. 89.

We adopt publicly a weapon-against-weapon strategy and concede that there are no targets in Soviet cities worth destroying at the cost of our own cities. At the same time, we emphasize that if the Communists start blasting our cities, we will use our hidden invulnerable forces to wipe out their cities. To make the decision easier for the Russians, we see to it that none of our cities or suburbs contain important military targets.[79]

Even if we can say that the Russians and the West have equal reason for policy decisions based on the judgment that "no matter what happens it doesn't make sense to start hitting cities," there stands in the background and in support of this the fact that in the nuclear age city destruction seems to be deterred only by the threat of city destruction in reprisal. Thus, McNamara went on to say, in his University of Michigan policy statement:

> The very strength and nature of the Alliance forces make it possible for us to retain, even in face of a massive surprise attack, sufficient reserve striking power to destroy an enemy society if driven to it. In other words, we are giving a possible opponent the strongest imaginable incentive to refrain from striking our own cities.

This question of continual massive deterrence, to which any consideration of limiting policy decisions seems inevitably to be driven, is my concern in the following section.

The Justice of Deterrence

In the foregoing, I have argued that the No-Cities or Counterforce plus Avoidance policy is the only just and sensible way to conduct war; that weapons analysts have sometimes overlooked the distinction between the unthinkable that has simply not yet been thought and the unthinkable that is un-do-able when thought about; that war as a trial of wills disconnected from trials of strength becomes an abysmal and unlimited conflict of resolutions; that current discussions of "general" war or "limited strategic war" need to distinguish more clearly between long-range attacks on strategic forces and strategic attacks on cities; and finally I advanced tentatively a gradation of policy decisions designed to set "firebreaks" between the steps in increasing violence, up to the No-Cities or strategic Counterforce policy. We need now to take up the moral and practical questions involved in "deterrence during the war," which at every stage seems necessary to keep war limited.

I shall argue that none of the virtues of the limiting policy decisions for which a case can be made, or of war considered only in the

---

[79]*Ibid.*, p. 97.

context of constant massive deterrence, can invalidate the distinction between the do-able and the politically un-do-able.

It is frequently contended that "both prudence and international law" permit and make it "desirable to carry out reprisals in kind," and that the only question remaining once an enemy strikes one of our cities is how to determine the equivalence to be exchanged moment by moment in countervalue war.[80] Whatever may be the rule of reprisal in international law today, this can hardly be said to settle the question of the justice — the natural justice — of reprisal in kind (or in *some* kinds). If it is unjust for an enemy to destroy our society, the fact that he does or tries to do so first cannot make it any less of an injustice for us to destroy his. William V. O'Brien's judgment concerning this "pernicious institution of reprisals" seems to me to be irrefutable:

> Few rights are more solidly established in the law of nations than the right of reprisal, and few principles have done so much to gloss over immoral behavior with an aura of legality. . . . This exceptional right [of reprisal in kind] applies to all the laws of war. It is supposed to serve two purposes: it provides a sanction for the law and it tends to restore the balance upset when one belligerent uses illegal means.
> Obviously, this kind of "legality" is ridiculous. . . . If bombing cities were really contrary to the law of nations, violation of the law could not affect the legal obligation to refrain from such bombings.[81]

Such a law of reprisals can only be described as a product of an age of legal positivism where justice has become something men and nations "make." No wonder they suppose they can make "just" an act that before was "unjust," or unjust when *first* done. With no sense of the difference between the do-able and the intrinsically un-do-able, the nations may well agree that a certain weapon or plan of war should never be used, unless, of course, it is. That excuse must today be called radically into question.

It can be shown that the traditional limits upon the "just" conduct of war were a product not so much of man's sense of justice as of "social charity" determining, in crucial situations in which the use of force cannot be avoided, how force can be directed to the saving of human life.[82] From this point of view — from the point of view of concrete Christian charity — even more than in the context of the natural justice surrounding killing in war, this so-called law of reprisal in kind, if it is proposed as a sovereign and all-embracing rule for conduct, must

---

[80]Thornton Read, "The Proposal to Use Nuclear Weapons Over One's Own Territory," (unpublished ms.) p. 28.

[81]"Nuclear War and the Law of Nations," in *Morality and Modern Warfare* (ed. by William J. Nagle). Baltimore, Md.: Helicon Press, 1960, p. 140.

[82]See my *War and the Christian Conscience*, chapter three on "The Genesis of Non-Combatant Immunity."

itself always be condemned. Pure reprisal between persons or between nations will appear especially heinous to a just or Christian man. Neither in inter-personal nor in international relations will a Christian accept the reduction of moral and political agency to this attempt to gain an empty victory of one will over another. Instead, if he is properly instructed and sensitive to the requirements of a love-informed justice, he is apt to call such punishing reprisal of will against will the very epitome of sin and of injustice.

The injustice of the law of reprisal is perhaps hidden from view in impure cases where actually *doing* the reprisal in kind seems clearly connected with accomplishing some definite purpose. In this way an almost self-enforcing system of diplomatic immunity is maintained, and restrictions are imposed upon the travel of Soviet citizens in this country roughly equivalent to those imposed upon American citizens traveling in Russia. Almost all the laws of war in the past have been enforced, to the extent that they have been enforced, by creating the expectation of reprisal in kind. The race toward increasing irreconcilability between actions of nation-states seems to be slowed down by *doing,* on occasion, the expected reprisal in kind, even if in itself the action has no reconciling power.

But then, it ought to be observed that many of these enforcements, which seem to warrant reprisal in kind, involve actions which are not *malum in se.* In a great many kinds of action the nations can "make" right what they want to, and enforce rules they agree to by reprisals in these kinds. What was not inherently wrong when first done but only legally proscribed, can be legitimately done in reprisal. The possibility of massive nuclear retaliation against the society of an enemy who struck first has made clear that the rule of reprisal in kind was never an all-embracing rule for the conduct of men or nations. *This* kind of reprisal can only be justified by a very immoral "moral" system, or by a positivism that seeks to "make" right in the second place what was ruled to be wrong in the first.

To the argument from justice and the argument from charity may now be added a third argument against ever *doing* the reprisal in kind that is now in question. Today the irrationality and purposelessness of pure punishment is laid bare, and the spiritualization of war into a contest of resolves is exposed as the most *abysmal* of all wars we could contemplate. One can still contemplate it, but it cannot be done except as an act that no longer has political purpose. Such reprisal would be a choiceless choice, an act without a definite end to be attained. For it can no longer be said that reprisal in kind — the kind we are speaking about — will "restore the balance when one belligerent uses illegal

43

means," or defend freedom or civilization, or hold back from destruction any life worth living, or even that it will enforce a lower limit of warfare.

It remains only to be asked whether actually *carrying out* this reprisal in kind is really necessary in order to "provide a sanction" for the lesser laws and rules of warfare which it is urgently necessary for the nations of the world to impose on themselves and one another.

Clearly, staged limitations upon the conduct of war, each stage separated from another by a "firebreak," depend on deterrence during war, and finally upon the hidden and not so hidden *possibility* that one's own cities may come into range. The threat that one's society as a whole and that of the enemy may be subjected to capital punishment seems necessary at the crucial point, to support the rule against the capital punishment of any society as a means of war, and to insure that this limitation is observed.

Shall we say this is to be compared to what must be done by any society which wishes domestically to abolish capital punishment for crimes? An exception has to be made in the case of treason in wartime and in the case of anyone who in resisting arrest shoots a policeman in his execution of the law. He has not only killed a man; he has also challenged the whole structure of the law, and precisely that law which seeks to order human relationships without capital punishment. For that, capital punishment is not likely to be abolished. Shall we say, then, that the nation which resorts to bombing without avoiding civilian damage as much as it can and instead begins deliberately to strike cities has challenged the laws of civilized conduct in war at such a fundamental point that such a society can be justifiably put to death? That nation has, in fact, violently attacked not only another whole people, but also a central part of the whole system by which, it is hoped, counter-society warfare can be abolished now that it has been invented. Is it not just, then, to exact the supreme penalty under these circumstances?

The objection to this line of reasoning, and one that is fatal to it, is that the analogy does not hold. In the case of enforcing the law, even the law which has abolished capital punishment, by *carrying out the deterrent threat* maintained in the minds of potential "cop-killers," the one put to death is the person who threw down the gauntlet to the whole administration of justice. In the case of strategic warfare against a whole nation, however, to do this would be to destroy indiscriminately people who were not "unjust aggressors" as a means of getting at their government (which, in turn, is now a useless endeavor). If this is like anything in the world, it is like shooting the children of the criminal who shot a policeman, or of a soldier who turned traitor in wartime. John Bennett's conclusion here seems to me unavoidable: "We must not deceive ourselves into believing that we could ever justify the use of megaton bombs for massive attacks on the centers of population of another country no matter what the provocation."[83] If a first strike, it would be both wicked and foolish. If a second strike, it would still be wicked and foolish — supremely foolish because when one comes to the actual doing of the act of reprisal in *such* kind it is already abundantly clear that the limitation upon war one hoped to "sanction" can no longer be preserved by the proposed sanction. It would be an act of pure purposeless punishment and retrospective vengeance. One simply cannot argue, as do the proponents of the various forms of limited war, that limited war must be *made possible* today and then say that illimitable inter-city warfare becomes less than an irrational absurdity *because committal to do this* is for the sake of deterrence *during* the course of limited war.

Any politically viable solution of the problem of war today requires that we finally employ a distinction between the *possibility* and the *certainty* of illimitable city destruction; and in deterrence during the war that we carefully discriminate between the *appearance* and the *actuality* of being partially or totally committed to go to city exchanges. The reader should recall at this point the discussion in the first section of this paper of Herman Kahn's contention (or admission) that while the appearance of irrationally inexorable commitment may have its uses, one would need in actuality and in advance to provide for revoking it. A nation ought never to be totally committed to action that is so irrational it can never be done by free, present decision; and even to *appear* to be totally committed may itself be altogether too dangerous. A nation ought not to communicate to an enemy that it might go to city exchanges without at the same time communicating some doubt about it, if it wants both to remain and to seem to remain a free agent with still some control over its destiny and the course of world politics. The *appearance* of *partial* commitment, or the *appearance* of *possible* commitment, may be enough of a commitment to deter an enemy.

I would be willing to consider adding to the stages of military decision set down in the previous section yet one more. A statesman might consider ordering one of the enemy's cities to be struck after a warning allowing time for civilians to be evacuated. That would be an act of countervalue warfare in which human beings have not been economized; and there may be some argument for it to be found in

---

[83]*Nuclear Weapons and the Conflict of Conscience,* New York: Chas. Scribner's Sons, 1962, p. 101.

the changed nature of much property today in comparison with the period when both civilian property and civilian lives were surrounded with moral immunity from direct attack.[84] Whatever be the correct judgment of this possibility, the arguments against ever actually engaging in a war of nerves by means of populated cities cannot be withdrawn. Deterrence will have to be accomplished by the deterrent effect of the *possibility* and the *appearance* of the possibility that the sanction of city exchanges will be invoked, or not accomplished at all.

I propose, first, to discuss the moral issues in preserving such a national posture, and to conclude with some remarks upon technical questions concerning the feasibility of limiting war under the deterrence of a possibility we do not intend to carry out. In approaching the moral issues involved in appearing to be willing to do something that is wrong, I shall make use of a volume of essays by British Roman Catholics[85] who follow the anatomy of the just war doctrine to a conclusion altogether different from mine, namely, nuclear pacifism.

It is never right to do wrong that good may come of it. Nuclear weapons have only added to this perennial truth the footnote: it can never do *any good* to do wrong that good may come of it. Neither is it right to *intend* to do wrong that good may come of it. If deterrence rests upon intending massive retaliation, it is clearly wrong no matter how much peace results. If weapons systems deter city exchanges only because and so far as they are *intended* to be used against cities, then deterrence involves a "conditional willingness"[86] to do evil, and evil on a massive scale. Granting that deterrence deters before or during the war, and that it supports peace or the control of war, that alone cannot justify it. It would be justified "if, and only if, in employing this threat, we were not involved in . . . *immoral hypothetical decisions.*"[87] The distinction between murder and killing in war, or between directly killing combatants and directly murdering non-combatants, posits an ethico-political principle that can only be violated, never abrogated. "Nothing, not even the alleged interests of peace, can save murderousness from evil",[88] and nothing, not even the alleged interest in deterrence during war for the control of war can save the *intention* to commit murder from being evil. Does reliance on nuclear weapons for deterrence hypothetically commit us, here and now, to murder, there and

---

[84]See Thornton Read: "Counterforce Strategies and Nuclear Weapons," p. 48 (unpublished).

[85]Walter Stein, ed.: *Nuclear Weapons and Christian Conscience.* London: Marlin Press, 1961.

[86]*Ibid.,* p. 23.

[87]*Ibid.,* p. 36 (italics mine).

[88]*Ibid.,* p. 36.

then?[89] If so, such deterrence is wrong, and can never be anything but wickedness. This conclusion would seem to follow from the comparatively simple moral truth that "if an action is morally wrong, it is wrong to intend to do it."[90]

This is surely a correct "finding" as to the moral law. The authors of these chapters, however, intermix with this a certain "finding of fact" which may be questioned. They assert that "deterrence *rests*, in the end, on the intention to use nuclear weapons," not that in some or many of its forms it *may* or *might* rest on either present murderous intention or on a "conditional willingness" to do murder. No wonder the conclusion follows: if this is the case, deterrence "cannot but be morally repugnant for the same ultimate reason as is the use of the weapon held in reserve."[91] The following statement of the case is a better one, and by accenting the first word the fact to be questioned can be stressed: "*If*, then, we find that 'having' nuclear weapons involves intending to explode them over predominantly civilian targets, no more need be said; this intention is criminal, just as the action is criminal."[92] This is the matter of fact that needs to be determined — whether it *is* so, and must or should remain so if it is now the case — before we can know how the moral prohibition of intending to do wrong is to be applied in an assessment of deterrence policy.

The authors of these essays systematically fail to show that there can be no deterrent effect where there is no intention to use nuclear weapons. They underrate what is pejoratively called "the argument from bluff," while admitting that if this deterred and if this is what deters there would not be an implied "conditional commitment to total war."[93] These essays are remarkably sophisticated, and at many points suggest their own answer. "Having an H-bomb," for example, is no simple matter. It is not only that "having an H-bomb," differs from having a gun "in respect to the nature of the object possessed." One can "have" one or both these instruments with subtly but significantly different ways of "having" them. There is then a considerable difference "in respect to the nature of the 'possession' of the object" that has to be taken into account.[94] The question of whether "possession" of massive nuclear weapons is reducible to the crime of "using" them over civilian targets, and the question of whether "having" or "posses-

---

[89]*Ibid.*, p. 125.
[90]*Ibid.*, p. 71.
[91]*Ibid.*, p. 78 (italics mine).
[92]*Ibid.*, pp. 73-4 (italics mine).
[93]*Ibid.*, p. 32.
[94]*Ibid.*, p. 75.

sion" implies a criminal intention to use them murderously, or a conditional willingness to do so, cannot be answered without first exploring a spectrum of "havings" that may be possible, and indeed desirable. This further exploration of the nature of the "possession" of nuclear weapons which may be possible will determine whether deterrence. by means of them before or during any war can ever be judged legitimate.

The technical possibility of deterrence before and during war can now be indicated, as can its compatibility with the moral prohibition of both the use and the intention to use nuclear (or any other) weapons in direct attacks on centers of population.

1. The collateral civilian damage that would result from counter-forces warfare in its maximum form may itself be quite sufficient to deter either side from going too high and to preserve the rules and tacit agreements limiting conflict in a nuclear age. In that case, deterrence during the war and collateral civilian damage are both "indirect effects" of a plan and action of war which would be licit or permitted by the traditional rules of civilized conduct in war. To say that counterforce strikes over an enemy's own territory are licit or permitted is to say that one can morally intend and be "conditionally willing" to engage in such a war. Whether one positively should ever do so depends on the conditions. Collateral civilian damage is certainly an unavoidable indirect effect and, in the technical sense, an "unintended" result of something a nation may and should make itself conditionally willing and ready to do. The deterrent effect, of which we are now speaking, is then, as it were, an indirect effect of the foreseeable indirect effects of legitimate military conduct.

One can certainly "intend" to deter in this fashion, and oneself be similarly deterred. Not knowing the tyrannies future history may produce one cannot say whether the one effect of successful resistance to them will justify the direct and the indirect costs. Still we foreknow that these costs may be very great indeed. This is to say that, at least to a very great degree, perhaps a sufficient degree, nuclear warfare is a design for war that is inherently self-limiting upon rational decision-makers without their having to intend to use these weapons directly to murder cities and civilians.

This is not at all a matter of "double-think about double effect."[95] To justify "possession" for the sake of deterrence one does not have to invent possibly legitimate uses for nuclear weapons, such as their use against a ship at sea. Many a military installation in the nuclear age

---

[95]*Ibid.*, p. 57.

is fifty or more miles in diameter.

2. In respect to the nature of the weapons we possess, there are two possible uses which cannot be removed. The dual use the weapons themselves have — the fact that they may be used either against strategic forces or against centers of population — means that *apart from intention* their capacity to deter cannot be removed from them. This means that there may be sufficient deterrence in the subjectively unintended consequence of the mere possession of these weapons. No matter how often we declare, and quite sincerely declare, that our targets are an enemy's forces, he can never be quite *certain* that in the fury or in the fog of war his cities may not be destroyed.

This is so certainly the case that the problem of how to deter an enemy from striking our cities ought not for one moment to impede the shift to a counterforces policy and to the actual intention to use nuclear weapons only against forces. We should declare again and again, and give evidence by what we do, that our targets are his forces rather than his cities. Since it is morally repugnant to wage war without renouncing morally repugnant means,[96] this should be speedily done, and communicated as effectively as possible to the enemy. Still, without any hesitation or ambiguity on our part, the weapons themselves will continue to have deterrent effect because they have ambiguous uses. They always *may* be used over cities; and no enemy can *know* that this will not be done. Was McNamara's reserved use of massive nuclear weapons for retaliation in case Russia strikes our cities really necessary, or his declared policy of conditional willingness to do this? Was not this aspect of his speech mainly needed to reassure domestic public opinion which is still so far from supporting any steps toward a counterforce strategy and away from pacifistic maximal deterrence?

Similar conclusions can be reached from an analysis of the "familiar spiral of reciprocal expectations" which is an important aspect of war in the nuclear age. This spiral not only threatens to be illimitable, but it serves as a built-in dampener, which no deliberate policy nor any intention can remove. This is the truth in T. C. Schelling's contention that in the nuclear age all forms of limited war raise the risk of general war, whether intended or not. The point here is not the "threat" of general war because of some technical or human failure or some mistaken calculation. The point is rather that in a nuclear age all war raises a risk of general war by an apparent *possibility* of a *politically irreversible trend.* War creates this risk which we share with the Russians. They can never "be confident that even the lack of resolution sometimes

---

[96]Cf. *Ibid.,* p. 82.

attributed to the United States could guarantee that general war would not result." "It is our sheer inability to predict the consequences of our actions and to keep things under control, and the enemy's similar inability [or our reciprocal doubt whether the other is in control], that can intimidate the enemy," and ourselves.

If war is no longer a matter of making no threat that does not depend on our ultimate willingness to *choose* general war, it is no longer a matter of having to put forth acts or threats that involve a conditional willingness to choose general war.[97] If war is sufficiently threatening, a good case can be made for the proposition that massive nuclear weapons should never be intended for use against societies. The nations of the world *should* and *can* devote all their attention and intention to making only just or counterforces war possible. A single great power *can* and *should* do this, since the other ominous possibility will always remain in the background as a shared and unintended threat.

3. Only now do we come again to the suggestion that the distinction between the *appearance* and the *actuality* of being partially or totally committed to go to city exchanges may have to be employed in deterrence policy. In that case, only the appearance should be cultivated. If the first two points above do not seem to the military analyst sufficiently persuasive, *or able to be made so,* then an *apparent* resolution to wage war irrationally or at least an *ambiguity* about our intentions may have to be our expressed policy. This is a matter, not of the nature of the weapons themselves, but of the manner in which we possess them — the "having" of them that is necessary for deterrence during justifiably conducted war.

The moralist can certainly say to the decision-maker that it can never be right for him to do such a thing as attack an enemy's society, or for him actually to intend to do so, or under any conditions to be willing to match his resolution against that of the enemy by means of populated cities. He can point out to the statesman that it can never be right for him to contrive to "make" the un-do-able intention irrevocable, or to have the intention of doing so. He can even point out where the military analyst will be found saying the same thing about the irrationality of total committal to an irrational act of war, or even of appearing quite unambiguously to be totally and irreversibly committed.

But the moralist must be careful how he rushes in with his ethico-political principles mixed with an assortment of findings of fact and various arguments *ad horrendum.* He must be careful how he spells

---

[97]See T. C. Schelling, "Nuclear Strategy in Europe," *World Politics,* Vol. XIV, No. 3 (April, 1962), pp. 421-424.

out his *moral* guidance for deterrence policy. For, on a sound solution of this problem the security of free societies may well depend in a nuclear age which is also an age of "megacorpses,"[98] "deracination from humanity,"[99] and of "unparalleled moral landslide."[100] The moralist must be careful how he disparages the so-called "argument from bluff" to a morally licit form of deterrence; and he should examine whether the reasons *he* uses to dismiss this argument are telling *moral* ones or rather technical judgments he has gathered to fulfill a prejudice.

Some Further Questions

The crucial question for the moralist is whether deterrent effects that flow from a *specified kind* of studied ambiguity concerning the intention with which a nation holds nuclear weapons in reserve are *praeter intentionem* (besides or without the actual intention to attack cities) as surely as are the first two types of deterrent effects we have analyzed. To say and to act as if we might go to city exchanges is certainly a form of deception. But, if this can be done without intending to make irrational immoral use of nuclear weapons, and even with the intention that our weapons be not so used and with the intention of revoking what had never even the appearance of total committal, such deception cannot be said to be based on the criminal intention or conditional willingness to do murder. The first thing to be said then, is that the intention to deceive is certainly a far cry from the intention to murder society, or to commit mutual homicide.

The second thing to be said is in connection with the moral problem of *deception* in politics and in wartime. A moralist need not slur over the fact that in all sorts of ways deception may be an evil, just as he need not slur over the fact that the killing of combatants is evil (though certainly not wicked). But having said this, it must then be pointed out that there are deceptions and deceptions. Or rather, the word "deception" ought perhaps to be reserved for any denial of the truth to someone to whom the truth is due, or permitting him to gather from you a false or inadequate impression concerning the exact truth which, in some sense, "belongs" to him. If this is a fair statement of the moral rule, then an experienced finding of fact must be that there are many situations in both private and public life when withholding the "truth" or even communicating an inadequate representation of the "truth" is

---

[98]One million dead bodies.
[99]Walter Stein, ed., *op. cit.*, p. 31.
[100]*Ibid.*, pp. 125-6.

not a lie. Relative to this, there is a teaching of long standing in the Western tradition about the virtues of a military commander, to the effect that there is nothing wrong with his having military secrets provided he does not pretend that he has none. It would be extremely difficult to support the judgment that an effective reservation about the use of the weapons we possess, or an intention that they not be used over cities, in any sense belongs to an enemy, or that this information is due to be given him.

Finally, a moralist must raise the question of whether this truth is not owed to the people of an enemy nation, if not to their military commanders. In answer to this, it goes to the point to say that this may be necessary to save *their* lives as well as those of our own civilians. Or (worse than their death from the point of view of an ethics that does not place supreme value in mere physical existence) it may be necessary in order to save them (and ourselves) from a measure of complicity in their government's conditional or actual willingness to save them by doing mass murder, or from the *tragedy* (not the *wickedness*) of actually being saved by murderous intention (if a wrongly willed deterrent worked) and some of them from the tragedy of living on in a world in which their lives have been spared in the midst of the greatest possible wrong-*doing* by a government which in remote degrees of participation was still their own (if the shared intentional risk does not work). So the question resolves itself into the question of whether it is ever right to withhold the truth in order to save life, to save from moral wrong-doing,to save from sheer tragedy. Does the truth that might well be "fatal" in all these senses "belong" to them? Is it "due" to be given if it can be? Do we "owe" them a true report that will unambiguously quiet their fears by effectively communicating to them (if this *can* ever be done) that we have no intention of engaging with their government in inter-society warfare under any circumstances? I am so far from believing that one ought readily to justify this deception that it seems to me that the first two types of deterrence must, if at all possible, be made to work. Still, if deterrence were based on a cultivated ambiguity about our real intentions, and if "deception" in an objectionable moral sense would thus in some measure be perpetrated, it would still be an intent to deceive and not an intent possibly to do murder.

Perhaps we should say that we ought to be conditionally willing to strive for this ingredient in deterrence, that is, on the condition that it is necessary to deter and to save life. I do not grant to a physician any right to withhold from a patient knowledge of his true condition; but then I also do not believe that learning the truth about his condition can be demonstrated to be so nearly fatal as, in our present supposition, it would be for an enemy government and population to learn that we do not intend to attack people. A better analogy might be the following one. If you were trying to save a man out on the ledge of a building, threatening to commit suicide and to take you with him, would you withhold from him, and have an obligation to withhold from him, any blandishments, including "daring" him to join you inside for a duel to the death by "Russian roulette" at three paces, with no intention of ever carrying out this dissuasive dare or threat?

The military and political analysts I have consulted do *not* reject as infeasible the sort of "possession" of nuclear weapons for deterrence which we are now discussing.[101] If it is thought to be infeasible now, then the "system" may have to be studied and perfected so that it can be done. For this may be one of those customarily "unthinkable" things which, the more you think about it, will prove to be technically and politically "do-able." If needed, it should be developed in many a scenario. It is on balance, I believe, morally "do-able," as city-busting is not, however much you think about it. Whether this ingredient in deterrence can be adopted and exercised by a democratic society is, of course, a serious question. It requires of a people a mature "ethic of restraint, limits and silence,"[102] not moral protest always, much less punitive fury or he-man morality; and a reliance on the morality and rationality of their political leaders not to be expected or (on any policy decision not so crucial) desired in a free society. For this reason, if for no other, all our attention and intention should doubtless be directed toward adopting, declaring and implementing a policy of counter-forces warfare, with the deterrence that policy affords. This is the doctrine which should form the consciences of free men today; and if their consciences are thus formed, it may then be possible to add to counterforce policy this last type of non-murderous deterrence.

Then it may be possible to put, not nuclear weapons as such, but the inter-city use of nuclear weapon into a category by itself, so that, while the capability still exists, the intention to attack cities will recede into the background so far as not to have actuality. Things as strange have happened before in the history of warfare. Tribes living close to death in the desert have fought cruel wars. They even used poisoned arrows, and certainly to a limited extent they fought one another by

---

[101]Halperin, *op. cit.*, for example, develops at length the distinction between "communication policy" and "action policy."

[102]Cf. Kenneth Thompson in "The Nuclear Dilemma—A Discussion," *Christianity and Crisis*, Nov. 27, 1961.

means of direct attack upon women and children. But they knew *not to poison wells!* That would have been a policy of mutual homicide, and a form of society-*contra*-society warfare that would have removed the possibility of any more bloody cruel wars, not to mention peacetime pursuits. In refraining from massive well-poisoning, or in keeping that ambiguous, did these tribes, in any valid or censorable sense of the word, still "intend" to poison wells?